The Collected Issues of
Space Review
for the years 1952-1954

Albert K. Bender

SAUCERIAN PUBLISHER

ISBN: 9798663795593

ISBN-13:9798663795593
GTIN-14 :09798663795593

© 2020, Saucerian Publisher

Albert K. Bender (1921-2016)

Prologue

It is generally a good idea to return to the classics in any genre. This also goes for UFO literature. Rereading a book after ten or twenty years is a rewarding experience. You will discover new data and ideas you didn´t notice before. The reason, of course, is that you are, in many ways, not the same person reading the book the second or third time. Hopefully you have advanced in knowledge, experience, intellectual and spiritual discernment. A good starting point is to reread the contactee classics of the 1950s,in order to understand the deeper mystery involved in what happened during that era.

SPACE REVIEW was the official magazine about ufology established in in 1953 by Albert K. Bender. Bender made a series of discoveries, which led him to believe that he had finally found the truth to the UFO cover-up. He had planned to reveal his findings in the October issue of the *Space Review,* but before the issue was published, Bender was visited by three "men dressed in black," who had already read the unpublished report and confirmed his findings. The "silencers" as he called them, scared Bender to the point where he did not publish the report, but left a warning: "We advise those engaged in saucer work to please be very cautious." Bender then suspended publishing on his publication and dissolved the International Flying Saucer Bureau (IFSB).

Albert K. Bender (June 16, 1921 – March 29, 2016) author of the 1962 nonfiction book *Flying Saucers* and the *Three Men*, was one of the most influential ufologists of the 1950s/60s. He served in the United States Army Air Forces during World War II. He was obsessed with the UFO phenomenon and became a UFO researcher, founding the International Flying Saucers Bureau. In 1965, he founded the Max Steiner Music Society.

He founded the International Flying Saucer Bureau (IFSB) (the first major civilian UFO club in the world) in 1952. Although the organization was a success at first, he suddenly shut it down in 1953. Bender later told that in March 1953 he had been approached by three men in black. These men visited him in his house and communicated with him telepathically. He received a metal disk from them and instruction. He reported that he felt like he was being transported. These men apparently shared insights into the nature of UFOs. These men shared the origin of UFOs with Bender. Afterwards he became ill and didn't eat for three days. As a result of the visitation, Bender felt encouraged to share what he had seen with other UFO investigators, but was refused. Bender suffered frequent headaches after the three men visited him and his co-workers reported that he seemed scared.

His alleged experiences were recorded in They Knew Too Much about Flying Saucers by Gray Barker, Bender's IFSB associate. Bender's experience formed "the legend of the men in black." Bender did not speak of the event for nine years. In 1962, Bender wrote *Flying Saucers and the Three Men* to tell his own story. In the book, Bender recounts that the men in black were from another planet. Barker published his book. Bender went on to manage a motel in California.

Bender was not the first one, however, to report visitations to UFO researchers from men in black. Bender reported that he had a second supernatural encounter. He was visited by three shadowy figures. They did not touch the floor, but hovered above it. They told him that their human appearance was an illusion and that whatever information he told people about their visitation would not be believed. They supposedly told him that they captured people from Earth and used their bodies to disguise themselves.

These issues of Bender's *SPACE REVIEW,* letter size are one of the earliest serials UFO publications. Saucerian Publisher was founded with the mission of promoting books in Science Fiction. Our vision is to preserve the legacy of literary history by reprint editions of books which have already been exhausted or are difficult to obtain. Our goal is to help readers, educators and researchers by bringing back original publications that are difficult to find at reasonable price, while preserving the legacy of universal knowledge. This book is an authentic reproduction of the original printed text in shades of gray and may contain minor errors, and readers' pencil markings from the original scanned copy. Despite the fact that we have attempted to accurately maintain the integrity of the original work, the present reproduction may have minor errors beyond our control like: missing and blurred pages, poor pictures and markings. Because this book is culturally important, we have made available as part of our commitment to protect, preserve and promote knowledge in the world. These issues are an authentic reproduction of the issues of Bender's *SPACE REVIEW* for the years: 1952- 1954. Great, but unpretentious, these issues are extraordinarily rare symbols by themselves of what was going on in those early years of the modern UFO era. This title has the following issues: Vol. 1. No. 1; Vol. 2. Nos1,2,3,4; Vol. 3. Nos.1,2,3.

Editor
Saucerian Publisher, 2020

Space Review

VOL. I, NO. 1   October, 1952   Bridgepo , Conn., U.S.A.

FLYING SAUCERS OVER INTERNATIONAL HEADQUARTERS IN CONNECTICUT

Flurry of Sightings After Formation of IFSB

WASHINGTON, D.C. — During July and August there were unusual reports from our Capitol that saucers were picked up on the radar equipment at that location. The Air Force ordered jet planes up to chase these objects that caused "blips" to appear on the radar screen. No satisfactory solution has yet been decided upon. One scientist claims to have formed flying saucers in a test tube—but that's not definite yet, either.

———

NEW YORK CITY, N.Y.—Sightings were reported over midtown Manhattan after the news of the radar discovery in Washington, D.C. Persons seeing the objects claimed that they were of an orange color and oval shape. Within ten days sixty reports were made. All this took place in the latter part of July, but reports have still been coming in.

———

LOS ALAMOS, N.M.—An unidentified object was sighted over major atomic installations at Los Alamos. It was shiny and metallic, made a 360 degree turn and appeared for about 30 minutes. Jet fighters pursued but with no success. Occurrence August 2, 1952.

———

LANCASTER, CALIF. — Over the Mojave Desert—Two round reddish white lights were reported moving in the sky shortly before midnight. Jets investigated with no results. August 2, 1952.

———

SEATTLE, WASH.—Large meteorite object burst over Seattle, and after it fell apart there was an explosive roar. This happened during July.

———

MIAMI, FLA. — Eight saucers sighted by airline pilots over Chesapeake Bay. They were 100 feet in diameter, moving at 1000 miles per hour, and glowing like hed hot coals. July 16, 1952.

BRIDGEPORT, CONN.—It seems that the flying saucer occupants know of the formation of the IFSB and its purpose. Since the formation of the society numerous objects have been sighted over Bridgeport and surrounding towns. Previous to this there were no sightings. It may me only a coincidence but the officers of the IFSB do not consider it to be such. The occupants of the saucers may be looking for friends and have found them in the IFSB.

In Bridgeport alone a couple riding in their automobile in Seaside Park sighted a round ball-like object traveling about 3000 feet up and at a rate of approximately 200 to 300 miles per hour.

One of our own club members sighted an orange object, round in shape with a point in front. It came from the west and she lost sight of it in the sun. She sighted this object before she became a member of the IFSB.

In Milford, Connecticut about eight miles from Bridgepo , the police and thirty residents sighted a bright silver ball over Long Island Sound.

Silver objects that hung in the sky were observed in New Haven, Connecticut by aircraft ground observers.

The President of the IFSB is losing sleep nights hoping that he will get to see one of the saucers. If they decide to contact anyone he wants to be on hand for that occasion.

———

The President announces that branches of the IFSB will soon be in operation in England, France and Brazil. People have been contacted there and have shown wide interest. We hope to also have branches in Mexico, Italy, and Australia. We are already formed in two Canadian Provinces, Ontario and Quebec.

MAYFIELD, KY. — Strange object sighted by twenty persons. Bright orange and yellow color, 100 feet long, and with round nose and pointed tail. August 31, 1952.

DENVER, COLO.—Objects moving at 3000 m.p.h. were reported by a veteran airlines pilot over Denver. They seemed to be controlled objects of yellowish tinge. They had no light or glow. Occurrence—July 19, 1952.

CLINTON, IOWA—Three fishermen sighted an egg-shaped object, very bright, which moved in a whirling clockwise motion. It disappeared and reappeared before taking off. August.

SEOUL, KOREA—Crew members of United States bombers sighted mysterious objects over Korea. They were globe-shaped, bright orange in color and emitted an occasional flash of bluish light. July, 1952.

DAYTON, OHIO—In two weeks over sixty reports of strange objects were reported. June 17, 1952.

DODGE CITY, KAN. — American Airlines pilot sighted "bluish-white" star-like object. It was traveling at about 500 to 1000 m.p.m. This was sighted in August.

MADRID, SPAIN — Several hundred residents sighted three round, shiny objects traveling at tremendous speed. The objects left vaporous trails. August, 1952.

SALEM, MASS.—A Coast Guard photographer claims to have snapped a picture of three flying saucers in formation. The photo was printed in all leading newspapers on August 1, 1952.

LANSING, MICHIGAN — Yellowish-orange "things" hovered in the skies over Lansing. The objects varied in size from cigar-shapes to saucer shapes. July 29, 1952.

OGDENSBURG, N.Y.—Three silver-objects sighted in the sky about 20 minutes. Shape seemed to be round and in three sections. July 25, 1952.

WEST PALM BEACH, FLA.—Scoutmaster and three scouts encountered strange object in wooded area. Tried to investigate and were blasted by ball of fire. The object was shaped like a half-a-rubber ball, about three feet thick and high enough in the middle to permit a man to stand. He claims he knows what the object was, but that it was better for him not to go any further with his knowledge because it might cause panic. The Scoutmaster said that his hair was singed off and tiny holes burned in his cap. The grass and growth around the area was burned. Army is investigating. August 23, 1952.

ANCONA, ITALY — An object blazing as bright as the sun crashed into the sea off the Adriatic Coast. August 2, 1952.

FT. WORTH, TEXAS — A noiseless fast-moving form with a fiery tail, sighted near Ft. Worth. August, 1952.

CHEYENNE, WYO.—Two air base airmen reported seeing a large "flying saucer" object coming out of the east as a tiny dot, it grew larger and threw off a blinding light. It hovered over the base about 30 seconds and then took off to the west. August 9, 1952.

COPENHAGEN, DENMARK—A Lt. Comdr. of a ship claims to have seen a bluish-glowing triangle. Speed estimated at about 932 m.p.h. in southeast direction. Sept. 14, 1952.

SUTTON, W. VA.—A housewife and six boys investigating a report that a flying saucer had landed on a farm, were confronted with a 10-foot tall monster, with a bright green body and a blood-red face. The monster gave off an overpowering odor that made all of them vomit. The group ran off, they were so frightened. Investigation proved that only the odor remained—but what was it? Sept. 14, 1952.

MEMBERS: For more detailed information on any of these reports write to IFSB.— Please date all clippings mailed in to us, and let us know the source.

EDITORIAL

People reading the newspapers today take little note of the small articles that appear from time to time about the "flying saucers" or other strange flying objects sighted in the skies. They no doubt read them but only laugh or scoff at their authenticity. However, if these same articles were placed on the front page of any newspaper in blaring inch head-lines, everyone would be in a panic, such as was created by the Orson Welles broadcast of years back.

For many years now objects have been seen in the skies, but little heed has been paid to them. The earth has evidently been under observation of some greater power out in space. If they are human, they are undoubtedly far more advanced than we are here on earth. If space travel has been mastered by this super race they must be advanced to heights unbelievable by earthmen.

Recently scientists made public that it is impossible for people of other planets, if there be any, to travel the distance from any planet to ours. However, I do not agree with their very unintelligent opinion because they did not consider the fact that people on other planets may have found the way of preserving life. If it actually would take a period of years to reach earth in their spacecraft, what would a few years mean to them, when they could possibly live for eternity.

Can you imagine a scientist creating a flying saucer in a test tube. Wow! How far can they go with their theories. I wonder if these test tube saucers had any occupants.

A very intelligent theory by one of our own members has possibilities. He claims that the saucer-people may have discovered the fourth dimension. Having discovered this, they found a way of traveling that surpasses anything conceived by earthmen.

In my opinion, the U.S.A. has already sent a rocket to the moon with humans as passengers, but under strict secrecy. The general public won't know about it for a couple of years. It would be dangerous to reveal this to the public now, since one of the foreign powers is in a position to wage war or challenge us. The army did reveal sending up a rocket filled with mice, chickens, and a goat which reached 250 miles. The animals were unharmed.

In summing it up, it would be wise for the public to start turning its eyes and thoughts toward the heavens, because there is more danger lurking there than on the earth itself.

THE PRESIDENT GREETS ALL MEMBERS AND OFFICERS:

The President of the International Flying Saucer Bureau welcomes all members and officers into our organization and sincerely hopes that everyone enjoys their term with us.

AL K. BENDER

A NOTE OF WELCOME

It is indeed a pleasure to welcome you into our organization. We trust that you will find this first issue to your complete satisfaction and it is our hope that you will not hesitate sending us your comments—good or bad.

Remember, this magazine will strive to please you but without your help this cannot be done. If, at any time, you would like to send in any article, we shall endeavor to find space for it in some future issue.

MAX KRENGEL, *Associate Editor*

FROM THE ASSOCIATE EDITOR'S DESK

The mystery of the "flying saucers" will be eventually solved by calm, clear thinking individuals.

As of this moment, we have three different types of individuals giving forth three different theories on the subject. The first type believes that the saucers are objects from either other planets or from somewhere on our own. The second type believes that the objects sighted are merely some form of natural phenomenon, though unexplainable. The third type claims that the other two are suffering from hallucinations and are seeing things which do not exist. It is this third type of individual upon whom I desire to comment.

When one reads the names of some of the people who have gone on record as having sighted these objects, intelligent people find it difficult to lightly push them aside with the claim that they were "seeing things". Airline and Air Force pilots are people not normally subject to hallucinations about what they see in their sky. I cannot imagine anyone telling the pilots who have chased these objects that they were chasing something that did not exist.

It is my opinion that something is up there. Just what it is I would not presume to say. This mystery demands a solution and anyone who believes that it is impossible for anything to be there, even in the light of overwhelming proof by official and non-official sources, lay themselves open to doubts about their intelligence. They are not interested in proving one way or another just what it is people are sighting. They are saying, in effect, that since they do not understand what is going on, everyone else must be crazy.

Send all news and articles to:

INTERNATIONAL FLYING SAUCER BUREAU

P.O. BOX 241

BRIDGEPORT 2, CONNECTICUT

U.S.A.

SCIENCE FICTION
N E W S

★ ★

Alan C. Rievman

Latest S-F movie is "3000 A.D." reported to be very good. Tells of New York City in the year 3000 A.D. The people revert to savage state after an atomic war destroys everything.

Latest Galaxy Novels publications is "City in the Sea" by Wilson "Bob" Tucker. For an evening of enjoyment get this novel now. It is superb.

Also by the same author is the Science Fiction Newsletter which is published four times a year. For information, write to P.O. Box 702, Bloomington, Illinois. Highly recommended.

Another excellent fanzine is Science and Culture Magazine published by Stanley Crouch, Holly Circle, Sterling, Virginia. Excellent publication. Mr. Crouch is a member of our Council.

The United States Rocket Society, Box 29, Glen Ellyn, Illinois, publishes a very informative pamphlet entitled "Rockets". We urge all members of IFSB to join this society.

Latest S-F pocket book by Bob Heinlein is "The Green Hills of Earth". Another novel by the same author is due.

A. E. VanVogt has published a new anthology which is said to be as good as his previous work.

Grosset and Dunlap have put out a dollar edition of Isaac Asimov's book—"I, Robot".

"Double in Space" which is composed of two excellent stories by Fletcher Pratt, has recently been put on the market.

An article on flying saucers appeared in the September issue of True magazine. I might add it was very informative and proved a point to all that read it.

Franklin M. Dietz, Jr., of 156 West Main Street, Kings Park, L.I., N.Y., has decided to put his fanzine Science-Fantasy and Science Fiction on tape instead of publishing it. This tape is sent to all members of his society that own tape-recorders. Mr. Dietz is a member of our Council.

In my opinion the best of the S-F movies to date has been "Destination Moon". For one thing, it could conceivably happen in the near future and also because of the technical style in which it was done. Technical advice was supplied by Bob Heinlein.

One of the best anthologies available is "Destination: Universe".

For true stories of the strange, the unusual, the unknown the IFSB highly recommends FATE magazine, published monthly by the Clark Publishing Company, 806 Dempster Street, Evanston, Ill. The Editor, Mr. Robert N. Webster, is a member of our Council, so let's all subscribe to this wonderful magazine.

Just what you Flying Saucer Fans are looking for: SAUCER REVIEW, published by Elliott Rockmore, P.O. Box 148, Wall Street Station, New York. N. Y.

We will place any ads in this column for our members or officers that may have articles for sale, or otherwise. There will be no charge.

Subscribe to CONN-FAN, published by the Connecticut Science Fiction League. Write to 130 Vera Street, W. Hartford, Conn.

Any readers who might have something to add to this column, please send your comments to IFSB. Send us news of your Science Fiction Club activities.

MENTION "SPACE REVIEW" when writing to any of above mentioned publications.

MY THEORY
By I. F. S. B. Members

THEORY NO. 1—Submitted by Representative GAIL SPRAGUE, Wisconsin.

After reading all the material I could obtain on the saucers, I have come to the conclusion that they are from another planet. I have tried to find some other explainable reason for the saucers and was ready to believe that they might be figments of the imagination, balloons, etc., but when such reliable men as scientists and astronomers give vivid descriptions of the saucers which they spotted, I cannot believe this. Often people may mistake an object as a saucer but scientific men are not easily influenced by what they see.

I - - - do not believe that these are - - - something developed by Russia or the United States or hysteria, balloons, reflections, meteors, etc.

THEORY NO. 2—Submitted by RONALD GMYREK, Member from Minnesota.

I believe the flying saucers are truly from another planet, mainly Mars. I think that they operate by some form of magnetic force and that the beings inside are many years ahead of us, in intelligence, that is.

Some people just laugh 'at the idea of life on other planets. I don't see why they do this. After all, earth is "another" planet if viewed from another body and we are its inhabitants. I believe that the beings in the saucers are here mainly for observation and perhaps, communication.

THEORY NO. 3—Submitted by FRANK GARAY, Member from Connecticut.

I think the flying saucers are space ships built by a much more intelligent race than ours. I also believe that the creatures in these saucers, if any, are beings who come to our planet in peace. They probably describe our planet as "a planet of wars" inhabited by people who use their power for the destruction of their fellow men.

I believe that any race who has mastered space travel must have been in peace all their lives. So, when these creatures land on our planet they will come here in peace and it is up to us to be unafraid and to welcome them.

THEORY No. 4—Submitted by Representative DICK CAMPBELL, Indiana.

These objects are from another planet, which one is unknown. I think the planet is Venus for three reasons: (1) In most respects Venus is like earth in size and diameter. (2) Venus is the nearest planet during conjunction and the nearest in the solar system. (3) Venus always has a cloud covering the surface to prevent astronomers from seeing the surface.

THEORY NO. 5—Submitted by Representative RONALD KINNEAR, New York.

I believe that intelligent beings are aboard the saucer ships and they are making a complete analysis of life and progress on our planet. There is a great possibility that living conditions on this planet are highly suitable to intelligent beings of a less fortunate planet. I believe that the truth concealed by our government officials should be told to the people in a man to man fashion.

EDITOR NOTE:

In each issue the editors shall endeavor to allow one page for the theories of members of the IFSB. We will welcome any that you may send us for publication. If your theory is not published immediately it will appear in a future issue. All theories become the property of the IFSB and cannot be returned.

HIGHLIGHTS about REPRESENTATIVES

VICTOR ROOT, Rep. Illinois—One of our more active representatives flooding this office with clippings and news items. He is to be commended for active work in keeping us posted. Keep up the good work, Vic!

ROBERT R. RITTER, Rep. Tennessee—Informs us many strange aerial objects sighted in his state. Claims that many of the reports are due to natural causes but some may be actual spacecraft.

LOUIE MASONICK, Rep. Minnesota—Not too many reports of aerial objects in his state. Wonder why Minnesota should be different? Louie has sent in numerous clippings.

ALAN RIEVMAN, Rep. Connecticut—Our International Secretary is certainly doing fine work. Besides obtaining new members for us he has turned over to this office a batch of news reports. Has obtained the largest amount of new members and exceeds all other representatives to date.

EARL D. BROADDUS, Rep. Kentucky—At work rounding up new members. Suggests that members tune in to radio commentator Frank Edwards. He finds that Mr. Edwards seems to keep pretty well up to date on saucer reports.

BRUCE A. JENKINS, Rep. Michigan—Reports that August was one of the busiest months as far as flying saucer sightings were concerned and most of these sightings were later confirmed. He personally checked on fifty-three sightings in his immediate area.

GAIL SPRAGUE, Rep. Wisconsin—Sent in numerous clippings mounted on heavy cardboard and all were of great interest to the IFSB. Miss Sprague has shown great interest in the IFSB and we know that she will prove to be one of our best representatives.

J. RONALD ALBERT, Rep. Ontario, Canada—Wha happened? No reports.

DICK CAMPBELL, Rep. Indiana—Claims he has many friends interested in IFSB. We hope that they will be future members.

GILBERT E. MENICUCCI, Rep. California—Doing his best to get members for IFSB, and sent in clippings.

MARVIN KISOR, Rep. Wyoming—Sent in clippings in regards to sightings in his state.

DIANE BUCHANAN, Rep. Iowa—No monthly reports. Send in clippings.

We would like to receive personal data about our Representatives such as birthdays, anniversaries, vacation trips, weddings, etc. We will publish anything of interest to other members.

Let's get those monthly reports rolling in on time, and let's get some new members for the IFSB. For every new member, you get two months free membership.

DIRECTORY OF REPRESENTATIVES

CALIFORNIA—Gilbert E. Menicucci, 675 Delano Avenue, San Francisco
CONNECTICUT—Alan Rievman, 2634 Main Street, Bridgeport
ILLINOIS—Victor Root, 1329 S. Avers Avenue, Chicago
INDIANA—Dick Campbell, 300 North Walnut Street, Franklin
IOWA—Diane Buchanan, 910 West Main, Marshalltown
KENTUCKY—Earl D. Broaddus, 124 Peyton Avenue, Irvine
MICHIGAN—Bruce A. Jenkins, 210 Holmes Street, Eaton Rapids
MINNESOTA—Louie Masonick, Jr., R.R. No. 3, Long Prairie
NEW HAMPSHIRE—Ralph Melanson, Box 417, Durham
NEW YORK—Ronald Kinnear, Fourth Section Road, Brockport
RHODE ISLAND—Thaddeus W. Wenclawik, 5 John Street, Woonsocket
TENNESSEE—Bob Ritter, 114 Marne Street, Memphis
WISCONSIN—Gail Sprague, 622 S. 4th Avenue, Wausau
WYOMING—Marvin Kisor, Box 111, Farson
ONTARIO, CANADA—J. Ronald Albert, 41 Woodlawn Avenue, Ottawa

Above names will not be published again. Additional names in future issues.

LET'S LOOK AT THE HEAVENS

October 3rd, Harvest Moon; 11th, 3 A.M. Saturn at conjunction with sun (becomes morning star); 22nd, Before dawn, Ornionid meteors; November 1st, Hunter's Moon; 8th, 4 P.M. Jupiter at opposition with sun (rises about sunset); 9th, 10 P.M., Mercury farthest east of sun, prominent evening star; 16th, Before dawn, Leonid Meteor Shower; December 12th, Before Dawn, Geminid Meteor Shower; 18th, 5 P.M., Mercury farthest west of sun, prominent morning star; 21st, 4:44 P.M., Beginning of winter in northern hemisphere. Sun farthest South—at winter solstice.

(Courtesy of the Hayden Planetarium, New York City, N.Y.)

THE HAYDEN PLANETARIUM SHOW SCHEDULE

81st Street at Central Park West,
New York 24, New York

October, November—"The Earth in Space"
December—"The Star of Bethlehem"

"ESCAPE"

by Akben Dem

"So, you dismissed all the workers today, Professor?"

"Yes, the job is completed and we are ready to take off at one A.M."

"One A.M.! But, Professor, you promised to take all those people with us and now they are all—"

"I know! I know! But I've changed my mind. Without them we can carry that much more food and supplies so that we will be able to survive that much longer on the planet Nao. Why should we worry about the others, let them perish in their atomic wars. The bombs are getting closer by the day. You can feel the vibration and the skies are darkened with the destruction they have wrought. Sooner or later someone will discover our secret. We cannot linger any longer. It must be at one A.M. or NEVER, this planet is doomed to destruction by a vast chain reaction."

"Professor, aren't you afraid that some of the workers may get suspicious and return to damage the ship?"

"No! Have no fear of that, I gave them a bonus plus their regular salary today. They will be celebrating tonight with the idea that it is their last night on this planet. We will be millions of miles away before they ever sober up to reality."

"Fine, but I think we should get some sleep. I'll set the timer to awake us just an hour before take-off time."

"Good! You go ahead and sleep. I'll take a last minute look at the ship before I try to doze off."

"Right, Professor, but try to get some sleep."

I suddenly awakened to a tremendous roar and the whole building shook. I thought at once that we were too late and that the atomic bombs had caught up with us. I reached over to wake up the Professor, but the Professor wasn't there. I raced outside—, the rocket was gone, smoke and dust covered the area. The Professor left without me. He never had any intentions of taking me with him. He wanted to be the only one to reach Nao.

As I staggered in a dazed condition back to the building, a sudden bright light lit up the whole grounds where I stood and a roar came from directly above me. The Professor was returning to pick me up.

A large shadow came down out of the sky not one hundred feet from me and before my eyes could adjust themselves, a large saucer-like object dropped to the ground with a terrific crash.

Steam and smoke hid the object from view, but after a few minutes two large figures stepped out of the mist. They were clad in suits made of a bright orange color, while over their heads they wore a plastic-like helmet. In every respect they resembled human beings, but they were almost six feet tall.

As they approached me, I began to back away until one of them spoke up in perfect English:

"We have come here in peace from our world. We wanted to escape the atomic wars there. Our planet was destroyed by chain reactions. We want a place to live and start anew. You see, we came from the sixth planet in the fourth orbit."

"Why, that's Nao!" I exclaimed in amazement.

"Well, you may call it that, but to us it was called Earth."

———

We will welcome any short-short stories from our members. All stories must be original and by a member of IFSB. Nothing will be returned unless you enclose a stamped, self-addressed envelope. Address all manuscripts to IFSB.

SAUCER SIGHTINGS BY IFSB MEMBERS

SIGHTING NO. 1—George D. Fawcett, Member of the Council, Mount Airy, N.C.

> Sighted at Lynchburg, Va., on July 6, 1951 between 8:25 and 8:29 A.M.
> Shape of Object—Round, half-ball, disk-like globe.
> Color of Object—Orange.
> Speed—Slow at first just after hovering and then gained speed.
> Peculiarities—No noise, no vapor or exhaust trail. Looked like another sun, hovered, zig-zagged.
> Height—About 225 feet high.
> Visability—For about four minutes.
> Direction of Flight—East to West.
> Size of the Object—Seemed size of large tractor tire.
> Report Made To—Wright Patterson Air Base; Civilian Saucer Investigation in Cal.

SIGHTING NO. 2—Dick Campbell, Representative for Indiana, Franklin, Indiana.

> Sighted at—Over Franklin, Indiana, about 3:30 A.M., July 28, 1952.
> Shape of Object—All three were disc-shape.
> Color of Object—Yellow-orange-red.
> Speed—250-300 m.p.h.
> Peculiarities—Just before it was over the small disc pulled directly under one of the other ships.
> Height—15,000 feet.
> Visability—For about three hours.
> Direction of Flight—South.
> Formation of Flight—In triangle.
> Report Made to—No one. Policeman next door saw same thing.

SIGHTING NO. 3—Barbara Knorr, Member Bridgeport, Conn.

> Sighted at—Bridgeport, Conn., on July 28, 1952 at 11:00 a.m.
> Shape of Object—Round with point on one end.
> Color of Object—Orange.
> Speed—Slow.
> Peculiarities—Did not move straight but in a half-circle.
> Height—Could not estimate.
> Visability—About one minute.
> Direction of Flight—West to East.
> Report Made to—Radar Tower at the Municipal Airport.

When sending in your reports on Saucer Sightings please give the date that the saucer was sighted. Do not put down the date that you make out the report. Thank you!

ARE SAUCERS HERE TO STAY?

by Earl D. Broaddus, Kentucky Representative

I started reading Science Fiction nearly twenty-five years ago. Anything that might possibly happen such as a visitor from another planet, or galaxy, I would be reasonably well prepared for. Don't get me wrong. I wouldn't be too surprised . . . but I sure would be as excited as a palsied Mexican jumping bean with the seven-year itch. Therefore, when in 1947 the saucer story hit the headlines I guess I more or less greeted the news as something I had been looking forward to for a long time, like greeting an old friend.

The many books and articles you see now concerning strange objects in the sky have caused quite a flurry of excitement to a lot of people, especially to those who have never discovered Science Fiction. Apparently a lot of the skeptics are gradually coming around to a point of asking a few explanations.

The Government has a lot of us wondering whether it is trying to protect the public or stick its head in the sand. Unless the Government has something new it can't talk about, but does know something about the saucers, I believe the time is about right for that little bit of information.

One of the most recent reports is the very interesting phone interview with Bill Squire by Frank Edwards, radio commentator. Bill lives in Pittsburgh, Kansas, and was going to work early one morning at radio station KOAM when he spotted this thing beside the road. Apparently it was hovering about ten feet above the ground. It seemed to have windows or ports and a constantly changing bluish light inside. As he drove up even with it and killed his motor he could hear a sort of pulsing sound coming from the thing. He said it was about seventy-five feet long and had a dull finish. As he pulled up and stopped, Bill said the thing took off straight up and made a sound that reminded him of about a hundred quail that had been flushed.

Naturally, all the reports and articles give you something to think about, whether you can believe all the stuff printed or not. Surely among all the thousands of words written there must be some bits of truth there somewhere. We can only hope so.

You can be sure that any visitors from outer space would be much more advanced than we are. This would necessarily have to be so or otherwise they would not be here. They would have had to learn to live together in peace. Something we have not yet learned. Perhaps they have had their costly wars but finally turned their efforts to finding out about the planet next door, or perhaps galaxy.

They would have solved their social problems and their economic headaches. A government would have been evolved that permitted a free people to develop to great heights of cultural and scientific perfection. A great race of people who perhaps remember costly mistakes they themselves made and see a threat to us as well as themselves by our clumsy tampering with power that our scientists can't even accurately measure. A power that some of these same scientists say might consume the earth once it is unleased; and perhaps a neighboring planet wiht it.

WE WANT YOU TO MEET

ALBERT K. BENDER, President, IFSB . . . Our President was born in Duryea, Pennsylvania, on June 16th, 1921. He left Pennsylvania nine years ago to move to Connecticut. He graduated high school in West Pittston, Pennsylvania, and is now about to receive a diploma in Industrial Supervision. He is, at present, Chief Timekeeper in a large industrial plant.

His interest in science-fiction started about ten years ago and has won him a host of friends. His interests do not stop at science-fiction since he also delves into the mysteries of the weird and supernatural. These interests become quite evident when one visits his home in Bridgeport. He has spent many long, happy hours in decorating his den with his own artwork. This artwork is not to be found on any of the "spicy" calendars one finds on the market, but rather consists of pictures of characters usually en only in bad dreams. He calls this pet room his "chamber of horrors".

The "flying saucer" mystery has led him to form the International Flying Saucer Bureau.

He owns a large collection of classical and semi-calassical recordings. His collection contains a vast number of unusual recordings which can be classified as rare. He is an ardent tape-correspondent and exchanges tapes with many individuals scattered throughout the country. His collection of science-fiction books and magazines is among the best.

Oh, yes! In conclusion, I must add that he is able to cook mostly any type of dish you can name. Personally, I never miss an opportunity of sitting down to one of his delicious spaghetti and meatball dinners, served on saucers.

ASSOCIATE EDITOR

(Next issue out January 2, 1953)

POST OFFICE BOX 241
BRIDGEPORT 2, CONN.
U.S.A.

Return Postage Guaranteed

To:

Space Review

Copyright 1953 by ALBERT K. BENDER

VOL. II, No. 1   January, 1953   Bridgeport, Conn., U.S.A.

IFSB OF BRITAIN ORGANIZES

Capt. E. L. Plunkett Appointed British Representative.

The IFSB has finally been organized in Great Britain with retired Capt. E. L. Plunkett, of the 8th Army as British Representative. Mr. Plunkett resides at 71 Chedworth Rd., Horfield, Bristol 7, England. Denis, son of Mr. Plunkett, is the assistant representative, but is now serving his country in the Royal Air Force.

Rep. Plunkett has shown great interest and foresight in forming the IFSB in the British Isles. Numerous articles have appeared in leading newspapers through his efforts. He is planning on using local halls and auditoriums to give lectures and show pictures with the aid of an edipiascope. He also plans to give talks at the local Toc-H club of that city which is a semi-war veterans type of society.

Many people in the British Isles have contacted Mr. Plunkett showing great interest in IFSB. Most of these people are very learned individuals such as officers in the Armed Forces, members of the British Inter-Planetary Society, Aero-Dynamists, newspaper reporters, and flying saucer enthusiasts.

At present Mr. Plunkett is holding weekly meetings at his home, where they discuss IFSB and flying saucers in general.

For further information about our British Representative see page twelve of this issue.

LUIS LUHRING NAMED PUERTO RICAN REPRESENTATIVE

Mr. Luis Luhring of Punta Santiago, Puerto Rico, has accepted the position of Representative for the island of Puerto Rico. He will handle all IFSB business in that place. Write to Box 23, Punta Santiago, Puerto Rico. Mr. Luhring is a very capable man and will aid the IFSB greatly.

FRANKLIN, INDIANA JOINS EN MASSE

Business Men and Public Officials Join IFSB. To Form Own City Group.

The City of Franklin, Indiana, has gone out fully for the IFSB and is now the only city in the world that has the most members in our organization. Through the great efforts and work of Mr. Louis Frahm, business man; Mr. Jack W. Moore, policeman; Mr. Robert Wolf, civilian defense director, and Mr. Dick Campbell, IFSB Representative for Indiana, this great accomplishment was made possible. At this publication, Franklin can claim 20 members with ten from nearly towns, giving a total of 30. Since all this interest has been aroused Mr. Frahm plans to form a city group with their own chairman, secretary and treasurer. Among the members you will find policemen, librarians, mechanics, commercial pilots, business men, bus drivers, students, etc. The group plans to purchase a telescope of suitable power. In addition to this they plan to rig up a $3\frac{1}{4}$ x $4\frac{1}{4}$ Graflex camera with an optical type view finder and screen door handle on each side for easy handling. This is the equipment they plan to start with. Later, if finances permit, they may build a radar set.

Franklin, Indiana, and nearby towns, have been fortunate in having had at least four sightings this past summer. Two were witnessed by Mr. Frahm and Mr. Moore. Reports of these sightings are reviewed in this issue of Space Review.

OUR PRESIDENT HEARS FROM PROF. EINSTEIN

Mr. Al K. Bender, President of IFSB, received a letter from Professor Einstein with this message: "Having no experience and only superficial knowledge in the field —I regret not to be able to comply with your requests." Mr. Bender wanted his opinion on the flying saucers. This was the Professor's reply.

SAUCERS IN THE NEWS

MAYAGUEZ, PUERTO RICO, Oct. 3, 1952—Strange objects were sighted by two persons in Mayaguez on Oct. 3, they were cruising East and were red in color. It was about 10:30 p.m. when they were sighted.

NORWAY AND SWEDEN, Oct. 13, 1952—During October the Norwegian Government stated that a strange object resembling a saucer landed on Norwegian soil. German experts are claiming that the devices are of Russian origin, and the description given by Norway fits the description given by German experts. Stockholm, Sweden, has also been sighting strange objects.

MELBOURNE, AUSTRALIA, Sept. 13, 1952 —A young woman sighted a noiseless green ball flying too fast to be a plane or a meteor. She said it smelled like a rotten egg.

STUTTGART, GERMANY, Nov. 1, 1952 — At the recent meeting of the third International Astronautical Congress in Germany where 200 scientists from 12 countries gathered they stated that saucers are not from Mars or any other planet. They said they are merely optical and atmospheric illusions.

LONG ISLAND, NEW YORK—A terrific air explosion took place over a small area of Long Island, N.Y., which broke windows, cracked sidewalks and caused general panic. There were no planes around or scheduled at that time, Oct. 1952.

INTERNATIONAL AIRPORT, NEW YORK, Oct. 16, 1952—A blue flame flashed over International Airport at 7:33 p.m. It was a fiery ball-like object. Hayden Planetarium official stated it may have been the fiery trail of a meteor.

TOPCLIFFE, YORK, ENGLAND, Sept. 20, 1952—During exercise "Mainbrace" RAF pilots sighted a white object at 15,000 feet. The object was silver in color and circular. It maintained a slow forward speed before beginning to descend, swinging like a pendulum. It followed the aircraft, revolved on its own axis at times, and then took off.

WASHINGTON, D.C., Oct. 16, 1952—The Navy announced that it launched rockets from giant balloons, high above the North Geomagnetic Pole, and sent them to altitudes of about 40 miles. The balloons were as tall as a 10-story building.

PARIS, FRANCE, Oct. 7, 1952 — A flying saucer was sighted over Southern France by two Air France pilots.

WESTERN KOREA FRONT, Oct. 29, 1952 —U.S. troops saw a half-dozen mysterious spark-throwing "cartwheels" over the western front of Korea. They were as the eye sees, 18 inches in diameter, moving in a 15-foot circle.

GAILLAC, SOUTH OF FRANCE, Oct. 29, 1952—For the second time in two weeks, 20 townspeople of Gaillac saw a series of white circular objects, slightly swollen at the center, spinning across the sky; they were flying in formation of two and were grouped around something that looked like a giant flying cigar. As the objects passed overhead they let fall a sort of string of bright white threads, which settled gently on trees and telephone lines. When the people tried to pick them up, they melted like ice. A police officer who picked up some of the thread said: "It looked like glass wool and it melted away almost as soon as it was touched."

OLORON, FRANCE, Oct. 17, 1952—About a dozen people, including a schoolmaster, saw flying saucers surrounding a long cigar like object flying through a clear sky at about 6,000 feet.

NEW ZEALAND—The clippings and stories from New Zealand are swamping our office and are so numerous that we must devote a whole page to them in our April issue.

For more detailed information on any of the above, please write to IFSB.

Please date your clippings that you send to us, and note the source.

SUTTON, WEST VIRGINIA MONSTER MAY BE
"COLLIER'S" ROCKET!

Rev. S. L. Daw, Washington, D.C., Representative, IFSB

I have personally photographed flying saucers six times and personally photographed the place where one landed in Charleston, West Virginia. I also talked to two eye-witnesses. I saw and talked to a police officer who was burned by one in Wheeling, West Virginia. My own cousin was the doctor who treated him.

I attempted to photograph one going over Melessa Pass, 5000 feet up in the Blue Ridge mountains, as I was at a height of 2500 feet at Wahala Glen just directly opposite from Melessa Pass. The picture was not too good due to the mist from the mountains.

The object that landed at Charleston, West Virginia was described as a large metal ball, throwing off a white light and after landing, two small men in red emerged from a trap in the top and climbed up a tree to look around. Seeing people watching them, they got back in and took off. We can prove what this was: In the attempt to shoot rockets to the moon, there is a device with the motors on the wings and the body of the device is a jet propelled apparatus which throws off a large metal shaped disc which throws off a red color from the center which when reflected could easily be taken for some sort of a small person. This was described in Collier's magazine of October 11, 1952.

According to the Washington Daily News, the monster seen at Sutton, West Virginia could be the rocket described in Collier's magazine. The picture on the cover of the magazine shows a sphere-headed, wide-bottomed, tank-bellied rocket craft spewing out burning hydrazine and nitric acid as it lands hind-end on the moon. The West Virginia people claimed to have seen: "An object estimated at 10 feet tall, four feet wide at the bottom and in the shape of a man. Two lights flashed from side to side, the machine made a noise like gas escaping, and a sharp sickening odor was about." Sounds somewhat the same.

The United States may be experimenting with something that the public is not aware of, and it is doing its best to keep it a secret. The age of rocket ships is just around the corner.

CIVILIAN SAUCER INVESTIGATION OF NEW ZEALAND
CONTACTS IFSB

The Civilian Saucer Investigation of New Zealand was set up in New Zealand on October 13, 1952. They plan to prove or disapprove the existence of saucers. It has no affiliation with the Government, the armed forces, or to any society to which its members may belong. Most of the members have been studying flying saucer reports for at least five years. They represent all interested parties, astronomers, scientists, aviators, and the man in the street. The committee consists of Mr. H. H. Fulton, a sergeant in the R.N.Z.A.F. attached to engineering, who is the President of CSI of NZ; Mr. R. J. Lavaris, a member of the Territorial Air Force, who is the secretary of CSI of NZ; Mr. G. H. Gilmore, aviation engineering inspector; D. Lavaris, a student studying for a science degree; and E. J. Greager, an astronomer and engineer.

Aims of the committee are to correspond with kindred bodies overseas, and to ultimately find the origin of flying-saucers and their comparison.

Mr. H. H. Fulton, and Mr. R. J. Lavaris have been made members of the International Council of IFSB. We hope to establish friendly relations with this society and get a representative in New Zealand. CSI sent to IFSB a large map of New Zealand showing all spots where saucers have been sighted with a history of each sighting. A complete report on this will be made in our next issue. We wish CSI of New Zealand the best of luck and hope they will be a success.

EDITORIAL

In 1492 Columbus discovered a new world after traveling thousands of miles across the great expanse of unknown waters called the Atlantic Ocean. It was a great adventure, yet one that was laughed at, ridiculed, and even spoke of as a "folly".

Here was a small group of men searching for what lay beyond the known, endeavoring to unfold the mysteries of lands that were not supposed to exist. All they had were three small ships laden with provisions that they estimated would last the journey.

The seas were infested with monsters, so the skeptics said, and the world was flat with a dropping off place. Columbus proved these fallacies to be wront, when he landed in the West Indies.

The years directly ahead of us will see another great adventure such as this. A small group of men will assemble in a certain designated place, climb into their ship, a ship vastly different than that of Columbus's time. This ship will be a rocket shop, and its occupants will shoot off into the vast sea of space to find new worlds, new peoples, and new frontiers.

They will be laughed at, they will be ridiculed, and the whole thing will be called the greatest "folly" on earth, but will it be such? Time has proven that impossibilities become realities,—the automobile, the airplane, radio, telephone, telegraph, television and the smashing of the atom are definite proof. All is possible to one who believes,—and I am a sound believer!

FROM THE ASSOCIATE EDITOR'S DESK

The mysteries of space have long fascinated most people on earth. One need not b an astronomer to gaze in awe at the sight which unfolds before the eyes as we gaze skyward on any clear night.

The vastness of space is difficult to explain, even for astronomers. When distances are spoken of it is simpler for learned men to use the term "light years" than miles. The number of celestial bodies suspended in space like our own earth are unknown. The guesses are from millions on up. But they remain just that—guesses.

We, who make our home on a mere cinder of matter in the eyes of space, cannot be naive enough to think that intelligent life exists only here. Those who believe that there is a purpose for everything which happens, should agree that these millions of bodies in space must serve more of a purpose than just twinkling brightly on a clear night.

Published quarterly by Albert K. Bender, Editor; Max Krengel, Associate Editor; Printed by Reliable Press, Bridgeport, Conn. Subscription Price: four issues, to members, $1.00; to non-members, $1.40 per year. Individual copies $.35. Exclusive publication of the IFSB, P.O. Box 241, Bridgeport 2, Conn., U.S.A. Send all news and articles to this address.

SCIENCE FICTION NEWS
Alan C. Rievman

Victor Root, Illinois Rep. of IFSB, has some Science-Fiction mags for sale, or free in exchange. He is selling them for a small fee. Write to IFSB for address.

The DECEMBER, 1952, issue of FATE magazine is a must to all IFSB members and officers. It contains an article by Curtis Fuller, entitled, "Let's Get Straight About the Saucers." A complete detailed story of the incident of the scoutmaster described in our January issue, is discussed with a picture of the scoutmaster. SUBSCRIBE TO FATE MAGAZINE AND KEEP UP TO DATE ON THE SAUCERS. Write to 806 Dempster Street, Evanston, Illinois.

New Pocket Books on Stands: Dell No. 627, "When Worlds Collide" by Philip Wylie and Edwin Balmer. Pocket Book No. 908, "New Tales of Space and Time", edited by Raymond J. Healy.

Thanks to Ray Palmer for our letter in the December issue of "Other Worlds". Clark Publishing Co., 806 Dempster St., Evanston, Illinois. Let's subscribe.

NEW BOOK BY VIKING PRESS: "Across the Space Frontier", edited by Cornelius Ryan, $3.95, Viking, New York.

RANDOM HOUSE HAS DONE IT AGAIN WITH: "By Space Ship to the Moon", written by Jack Coggins and Fletcher Pratt, foreword by Willy Ley. $1.

SCIENCE FICTION NEWS-LETTER, by our Council Member, "Bob" Tucker, P.O. Box 702, Bloomington, Illinois.

THE UNITED STATES ROCKET SOCIETY, Box 29, Glen Ellyn, Illinois.

Hollywood is coming out with two good movies: "War of the Worlds" and "The Conquest of Space".

SAUCER REVIEW, by Elliott Rockmore, a member of our Council. P.O. Box 148, Wall St. Station, New York 5, N.Y.

Owners of tape recorders or wire recorders: Join T.R.I. (Tape-respondence International. Send your voice to your correspondents) 3488—22nd St., San Francisco 10, Calif.

BORDERLAND SCIENCES RESEARCH ASSOCIATES located at 3524 Adams Ave., San Diego 16, California, would like to have IFSB members join their society.

Many new Science Fiction Mags are hitting the newsstands and some are good while others are the usual run. A few of the better ones are: Tops in SF; Science Fiction Quarterly and Fantastic.

Two good S-F books: "Robots Have No Tails" by Lewis Padgett and "Player Piano" by Kurt Vonnegut. Both humorous line.

The officers of IFSB are planning on issuing a 12-page booklet sometime next year with a complete record on all saucer reports that they now have collected. This booklet will not be a regular issue of "Space Review", but a separate issue and will sell for 50c to everyone. Our President, Mr. Bender, will write the foreword with comments throughout by official of IFSB. The booklet will be entitled IFSB REPORTS ON THE SAUCERS. If interested, write!

We would like members and officers to send in snapshots of themselves so that when the time comes for us to print pictures in Space Review, we will have the photos available.

MENTION "SPACE REVIEW" when writing to any of above mentioned publications.

This page will be eliminated in future issues, and will be replaced by articles on "saucers".

"MY THEORY"

by IFSB Members

THEORY NO. 6—Submitted by BARBARA KNORR, Member from Connecticut

Everybody seems to believe that the "saucers", whatever they are, come from this Solar System. I do not believe any other planet but ours can support intelligent life. Perhaps plant life, but not human.

I do believe tnat if our planet can support life, why not other planets in other Solar Systems. I do not believe that these people wish to destroy us because if they had they could have done so long ago. Also, how do we know that these things we see are not beings themselves.

THEORY NO. 7—Submitted by Representative LOUIE MASONICK, JR., of Minnesota

My theory is one most IFSB members seem to have. First, I believe they are from another planet. All those stars must have something going around them. All those celestial bodies must be up there for some reason, besides to look at. Then, also, they may even be from our Solar System.

I do not think an official agency of our government should come out and say—"we do not know what they are and whether or not they are a menace." The best way to reveal the objects would be through clubs like the IFSB. I do not believe that they are a menace. I think there is intelligent life on them and that they are just observing us.

THEORY NO. 8—Submitted by Representative ALAN RIEVMAN of Connecticut

My theory on the origin of the "flying saucers" is that they are definitely real and are from one of the planets of our Solar System. I do not believe that they are from one of the other Solar Systems. These "neighbors" probably thought that our planet could not have intelligent life upon it, but with the first atomic explosion they may have changed their minds.

I am sure that they are not from Earth because if they were ours it would be impossible to keep it quiet and if they were from a foreign government they wouldn't be flying over the United States. They would risk being shot down and their secret revealed to us.

THEORY NO. 9—Submitted by Representative VICTOR ROOT of Illinois

My theory is that the "flying saucers" are manned ships controlled and operated by intelligent creatures who are scouting our world. They will not try to make contact with us for many reasons. One is that we are too warlike and emotional. Another is that we have diseases which may harm or even kill them. Some day when we reach out and touch the planets we may meet them. A race of intelligent creatures other than ourselves, certainly does exist.

THEORY NO. 10—Submitted by ALAN STAZER, Member from California

I think that the "flying saucers" are from the solar system of ALPHA or PROXIMA CENTUARI. Most likely the 3rd or 4th planet. The planet is probably about 4000 miles in diameter and two-thirds as big as the earth. Some other reasons are that Centauri is too far distant for observation of such a small body as a planet. This star is of about the same size and the same spectral, type-GO, as the Sun. Editor's Note: WOW!

All theories become the property of IFSB and cannot be returned.

HIGHLIGHTS ABOUT REPRESENTATIVES

DICK CAMPBELL, Rep. Indiana—Rep. Campbell has written us many interesting letters and aided in making his home town of Franklin the only city in the world with the most IFSB members. At present it totals over twenty. He was assisted by Mr. Louis Frahm, and Mr. Jack Moore of that place.

* * *

J. RONALD ALBERT, rep. Ontario, Canada—Will be appointed Representative of CANADA AT LARGE. Doing a fine job. Would like more Canadians to join club.

* * *

VICTOR ROOT, Rep. Illinois—One of our most valuable representatives. He has spent much time preparing a map of the United States showing the places where saucers have been sighted. He is quite a poet, too; see his poem in this issue. Mr. Root presented the IFSB with this saucer map. We are proud of it. We are sorry to say that Mr. Root may have to move to California in the near future. It will be very hard to replace such an ardent worker.

* * *

EARL D. BROADDUS, Rep. Kentucky   Obtained two new members for IFSB. One of these members, a Mrs. Glenn C. Fuller, saw a flying saucer. Her report will be in our next issue of "Space Review". Mr. Broaddus is spreading the word about IFSB.

* * *

DIANE BUCHANAN, Rep. Iowa   Obtained a new member, and has clippings she intends to send in to IFSB.

* * *

GAIL SPRAGUE, Rep. Wisconsin—Gail is quite the cartoonist. She sent in a cartoon for us which really made the International Staff roll off their chairs. She showed the parlor of a home with the front door open, a strange looking creature had walked in the door leaving muddy tracks on the floor. Outside can be seen a saucer parked on the lawn. A housewife approaches the creature and this is what she says: "I don't care where you're from. Look at my clean rug.'" She also sent us a fine poem that appears in this issue. Gail obtained a new member for us also. She sure is showing fine interest.

* * *

ALLAN LEVINSKY, Rep. Maine—Claims that very few people are seeing saucers in Maine. Is doing his best to get people interested in IFSB.

* * *

ROBERT R. RITTER, Rep. Tennessee—Chalks up another member for IFSB

* * *

LUIS LUHRING, Rep. Puerto Rico—Mr. Luhring has sent us numerous clippings from Puerto Rico about saucers. He plans to get as many people as possible to join IFSB. He says that the interest in saucers is as great in Puerto Rico as anyplace else.

* * *

S. L. DAW, Rep. Washington, D.C.—We are happy to have for our representative in Washington, D.C., the first member of the clergy, Reverend Daw. Mr. Daw, as he prefers to be called by club members, is doing great work for IFSB. We are anxiously awaiting to see his actual photos of saucers, that he took himself.

* * *

RONALD KINNEAR, Rep. New York—Took upon himself to advertise in his own state and had 50 post cards printed and plans to mail them out, in his state.

* * *

We are not getting any reports from some of our Representatives. It is absolutely necessary that we hear from you, so please do your best to get those monthly reports rolling in on time.

DIRECTORY OF REPRESENTATIVES

The following are additional representatives since our last publication.

BRITISH REPRESENTATIVE—Edgar L. Plunkett, 71 Chedworth Rd., Horfield, Bristol 7, England; Assistant Representative for Britain—Denis Plunkett

PUERTO RICAN REPRESENTATIVE—Luis Luhring, Box 23, Punta Santiago

COLORADO—Verna M. Hampton, 4245 Alcott St., Denver

MAINE—Allan Levinsky, 59 Atlantic St., Portland

MISSOURI—Ralph Hetzel, 6 Scarsdale, St. Louis 17

NEW JERSEY—August C. Roberts, 443 Ogden Ave., Jersey City

NORTH CAROLINA—David T. Benton, Box 430, E.C.C., Greenville

OHIO—Robert C. Schnelle, Sr., 714 McMakin Ave., Cincinnati

OREGON—G. L. McColly, 524 Jersey St., Silverton

DISTRICT OF COLUMBIA—Rev. S. L. Daw, 5119—7th St., N.W., Washington

WEST VIRGINIA—Gray Barker, Box 981, Clarksburg

Above names will not be published again. Additional names in future issues.

Anyone that wishes to correspond with other members will please send us permission to print your name and address so that others will know that you desire correspondence. We do not publish lists of our members' names and addresses without permission from them.

LET'S LOOK AT THE MAGAZINES

READERS DIGEST FOR JULY 1952—Two articles: "Have We Visitors from Space," and "Flying Saucers—New in Name Only."

TRUE MAGAZINE, SEPT. 1952—"The Flying Saucers and the Mysterious Little Men."
OCT. 1952—"We Flew Above Flying Saucers."
DEC. 1952—"What Radar Tells About Flying Saucers."

QUICK MAGAZINE, OCT. 20, 1952—"Moonbound," Page 18.

COLLIER'S, OCT. 18, 1952—"Man on the Moon."
OCT. 25, 1952—"More About Man on the Moon."

PIC MAGAZINE, NOV. 1952—"How Do Saucers Fly?"

SIR MAGAZINE, DEC. 1952—"Flying Saucers and the Air Around Us."

MR. MAGAZINE, JAN. 1953—"Is Washington Afraid of Flying Saucers?"

MAN TO MAN MAGAZINE, JAN. 1953—"Flying Saucers Are Not New."

THE MYSTERY OF OTHER WORLDS REVEALED—A Fawcett Book No. 166. Excellent. A four star edition—one of the finest to date in the pulp line. Cost 75c. We advise all saucer-minded folk to get this magazine. It is only once in a great while that a publisher puts out such a fine publication. Contains news of Space Travel; Flying Saucers; and Rocket Development.

These magazines are in the IFSB LIBRARY as part of our collection. We will send written information to anyone that may have questions on above magazines.

Coming in April "SPACE REVIEW"—"SAUCERITIS" by John Armitage of England. An article that will make you really THINK!
A COMPLETE LISTING OF ALL OF OUR OFFICERS AND COUNCIL MEMBERS

TO ALL MEMBERS OF THE I.F.S.B.—
GREETINGS FROM ENGLAND
Capt. Edgar L. Plunkett, British Representative

Are we on the verge of a breath-taking discovery? Yes, I believe we really are! To quote Captain Eddie Rickenbacker, "Too many good men have seen Flying Saucers for us to dismiss them lightly as hallucinations."

The nineteenth and twentieth centuries have produced a number of astonishing discoveries notably the dreaded atom bomb, and also has had to discard in many cases previously held convictions such as that "matter is indestructible".

Even the average layman today, due to increased educational facilities, and access to literature of all kinds, has a very good idea that life in all its forms consists of "energy", and that this energy somehow links back to some form of pulsating orbital structure like unto the universe, but on an infinitesimally smaller scale. Therefore, it is—to me at least— quite believable that it is possible that somewhere—something—someone—has solved the riddle of this energy, etheric, electromagnetic, call it what you will. Having progressed so far, it follows that given elements capable of withstanding immense stresses and strains, the propulsion of what has become known as the "Flying Saucer" becomes a possibility. It is known that between the Sun, Moon, and our Earth, and presumably between other inter-planetary and possibly interstellar bodies there exists magnetic lines of force, thus if some form of aircraft or saucer has control of the means of attraction and repulsion, these lines of force which by the way never touch one another, would form the perfect highway along which to travel at the speed of light, and probably very much faster. It would also account for the capability of these so-called "saucers" to accomplish right-angled turns, inasmuch that these known magnetic waves emanate in all directions. Therefore, from the point of view of the average thinking man in the street, I say, "I believe the flying saucer does exist, and that the coming years will vindicate such men as Captain Mantell, Kenneth mold, and countless other pioneers in this field." In conclusion, may I say to all IFSB members at home and abroad, "carry on the good work, and above all, do not be disappointed, discouraged or deluded by the jeers and sneers of the ignorant so-called majority."

The best of everything for the New Year ahead!

Yours fraternally,　　E. L. PLUNKETT

MYSTERIOUS CRAFT
by Gail Sprague

Out of the dark, mysterious, depths of
　　space,
Came strange looking craft at a tremen-
　　dous pace.
Their course was true, the third planet
　　from the sun,
Their orders: Don't return until your task
　　is done.
Down they descended; some got out.
"Be back in 24 hours," the commander
　　told the scout.
Time went fast, all returned.
Off went the craft, bearing all they'd
　　learned.
The decision was reached, never again,
On this small planet they'd ever land.
Wars, corruption, prejudice and greed,
Made this the worst of all planets, all
　　agreed.

OUT THERE
by Victor Root

Out in space lies my destiny,
Out there, beyond the clouds;
Where winds have not yet blown,
Where man has not yet gone;
That's where I long to roam.

Out in space lies my destiny,
Out there, among the stars;
Where night is forever ruling,
Where solitude is soothing;
That's where I long to roam.

Give me a silver ship,
To make the happy trip;
Out there; among the stars.

SAUCER SIGHTINGS BY IFSB MEMBERS

Exclusive! From Franklin, Indiana and Surrounding Towns

SIGHTING NO. 4—On the morning of July 28, 1952 in the skies to the southeast and at times directly over Franklin, Indiana appeared three strange objects. Their flight was watched by a large number of men of sound mind and character. The following is compiled from a Police report turned in by Capt. Lee Sloan, Patrolman Jack W. Moore and Patrolman Kenneth Rund of the Franklin, Indiana Police Department on Monday morning, July 28, 1952 at 6:00 a.m. These objects were witnessed by policemen, civilian authorities, and members of the United States Army. After notifying all proper authorities of the objects no definite steps were taken by the army or otherwise. The report is as follows:

There were three objects, one larger and brighter than the two smaller objects. The larger of the three seemed to cast off a white yellowish light. Its pattern of flight seemed to be that of a circle. It seemed to always be keeping track of the two smaller objects. The two smaller objects cast off a distinctive light of their own, one being an orange hue and the other a reddish color. The two smaller ones seemed to be in a dog fight all their own, since they executed barrel rolls, loops and spins. They made turns of 90 degrees and 45 degrees without losing any degree of speed, as well as dancing up and down as if someone was playing with a giant "yo-yo". The objects made single sorties to the south completely out of sight, to return almost immediately into view again, joining the other in a neatly executed show of turns, loops and spins. We estimated their height at approximately 15,000 feet, while their speed varied from an estimated 1500 miles per hour to an estimated 10,000 miles per hour. Even with a pair of binoculars it was almost an impossibility to determine any exact shape other than that they appeared to be round and flat as a saucer. They were observed for a period of four hours and fifteen minutes. Dawn came at 4:48 a.m. and all stars had gone around 5:00 a.m. At 5:03 a.m. it was bright day, light—and the three objects were still visible. Their color did not change in daylight. At 5:11 a.m. the larger of the three objects was joined by the two smaller ones; the smaller objects one at a time disappeared above the larger, first the orange, then the red. After seeming to envelope the two smaller objects it moved up and to the west out of sight. The joining of the three objects and the disappearance of the larger took exactly 40 seconds. These objects were verified by: Edinburg Police Dept.; Camp Atterbury, Ind.; Columbus Police Dept.; Seymour State Police Dept.; Greensburg Police Dept.; North Vernon Police Dept.; Connersville Police Dept.; Connersville State Police Post; Fort Wayne, Ind.; and Madison, Ind. Mr. Moore and Mr. Rund are IFSB members now.

SIGHTING NO. 5—Louie Masonick, Jr., Representative for Minnesota

Sighted a round object Northeast of Long Prairie, Minnesota about 2:30 p.m., April 20, 1952. It was a dull gray color, traveling about 250 MPH and when it ascended their was a low hum. It was about 5,000 feet high, and was visable for about 45 seconds. Direction of flight was from East to West in one direct path.

SIGHTING NO. 6—Alan K. Stazer, Member from California

Sighted a disc shaped object in the East of Los Angeles about 9:08 p.m. on September 22, 1952. It was a yellowish white in color, and remained in a stationary position for about 4 seconds. It was about 12 degrees above the horizon. It was about 50 feet in diameter and traveling due north.

When sending in your reports on Saucer Sightings, please give the date that you saw the saucer. Thank you!

EXCERPTS FROM A SUMMARY OF A FIVE-YEAR
FLYING SAUCER INVESTIGATION

By George D. Fawcett, International Council, IFSB

I have just decided to stop investigation that I began a little over five years ago on one of the most fascinating mysteries of modern times, that being the well known "Flying Saucer" phenomena. Since the summer of 1947 when the first saucer scare broke out in the United States, I have spent much of my time, money and energy seeking a solution to this riddle. While carrying on my private investigations I was able to interview several astronomers, scientists, pilots and guided missile experts, who had spotted these saucers or at least had been investigating or studying these strange objects. In addition to these interviews I have talked to many eye-witnesses who had sighted these objects throughout the United States and have mailed questionnaires out to many others.

I have kept bulletins and scrapbooks on the saucers for the past five years, and while going to college I wrote a six-page pamphlet entitled "The Flying Saucer Phenomena" for my friends, teachers, and classmates. I have lectured to several groups in Lynchburg. Though I've been interested in this phenomena from the very first, my sighting of an orange disk-like globe which hovered for four minutes over the Lynchburg College administration building in Lynchburg, Virginia, on the morning of July 6, 1951, has increased my interest threefold since then. That is one of my reasons for stopping my investigation. It's really too big a job for one person to handle. We must realize that we are dealing with a phenomena that is as fantastic as it is fascinating. Many of the reports that I have been able to gather in my collection tend to back this statement.

Some recent thoughts about the "flying saucers" are that perhaps there will be some landings soon. This doesn't seem too far-fetched in that these flying saucers are still being seen everywhere, for longer periods of time, and in groups instead of alone, as well as more reports of huge saucer or rocket ships. Then, too, they seem to come and go at will, perhaps being stationed as satellites themselves.

I feel that our government must know something about these saucers because in my opinion at this very moment the United States Government is carrying on an educational program regarding interplanetary travel of our country. Perhaps space ships from other planets are already here! At any rate, whether they are trying to prevent religious controversy or panic or for any other motives which they might have, our government is still releasing, denying, suppressing and even plating reports at intervals for some reason.

Regardless, the future will tell! In closing, I'd like to use a favorite phrase of Charlie Lineberry, Lynchburg College student who said, "things are really looking up." I wonder if some things aren't looking DOWN, too; Sooner or later we're bound to find out, and to this all I can say is, "the sooner, the better."

EDITOR'S NOTE: Mr. Fawcett's discussions and opinions will be found in future issues of Space Review.

ATTENTION MEMBERS AND OFFICERS: If you would be interested in receiving an emblem to wear on your coat lapel with our club letters "IFSB" engraved on a Saucer background, we would be interested in knowing. We cannot order these emblems unless we get enough people showing interest. The price would be approximately $1.00 each. Please let us know as soon as possible. Thank you!

WE WANT YOU TO MEET

EDGAR L. PLUNKETT, BRITISH REPRESENTATIVE—Born at Bristol, Glos., England, on December 26, 1903. Covered most parts of the world as a radio operator at sea from 1922 to 1936, including the U.S.A., notably New York, Boston, Baltimore, Norfolk, Newport News, Tampa, Mobile, and many other ports. Has many interesting memories of the prohibition days, the gangster era, Jack Dempsey, Babe Ruth, Lou Gehrig and other notable highlights. Has worked for many years for Anglo-American friendship and still corresponds with friends here in U.S.A. Was called to service in 1939. Was rescued from Dunkirk Beaches by the French Destroyer L'Incomprise on June 1, 1940. Went to Middle East in 1941, and served through three Western Desert Campaigns with the British 8th Army. After fall of Tunis was commissioned in Palestine and was then posted in Egypt. Returned to England at the end of the war after four and a half years service overseas as a Captain. Now employed by his original firm as a clerk.

He has a wife and three children, their ages are Denis 21, now with the RAF, Diana 18, and Michael 14. Hobbies are writing and reading and other journalistic yearnings including poetry, plus an unabated desire to travel. Since the formation of Civil Defense a year or so ago, he has become a qualified instructor and lectures three evenings weekly to industrial personnel.

Mr. Plunkett has shown great interest in IFSB activities and will without a doubt prove to be our most valuable foreign representative.

ASSOCIATE EDITOR

(Next Issue—April 1, 1953)

POST OFFICE BOX 241
BRIDGEPORT 2, CONN.
U.S.A.

Return Postage Guaranteed

To:

FIRST ANNIVERSARY ISSUE

Space Review

Copyright 1953 by ALBERT K. BENDER

VOL. II, NO. 2   APRIL 1953   Bridgeport, Conn., U.S.A.

SAUCER PHOTOGRAPHED BY NEW JERSEY REPRESENTATIVE

On July 28, 1952, August C. Roberts, IFSB Representative for New Jersey, was fortunate enough to actually photograph a flying saucer over New York City. The photographs sent to our headquarters are authentic and copies are in our files.

Mr. Roberts visited Mr. Bender, IFSB President in Bridgeport, on February 8, 1953, where a thorough discussion took place.

The object photographed looked like a shiny coin. The figure was only a few thousand feet from the ground, and moving very slowly. It was of orange color, with reddish brown rim.

A copy of Mr. Robert's photo appears in the recent issue of "The Mystery of Other Worlds Revealed", Fawcett Book No. 166, on page 136. Copies of the photograph mentioned will be sent to any IFSB member desiring same. hese copies must be returned within one week after receipt due to the fact that they are only on loan. A certain deposit will be required on these photos while in your possession. This deposit will be refunded when you mail back the photos to IFSB.

VATICAN SAYS: SPACE DWELLERS MAY EXIST

Last November a Vatican pronouncement said: "Roman Catholics are free to accept or deny (the existence of space dwellers) according to their own points of view. The last word is up to experimental science. There is nothing else to do for the theologians but wait."

The article is signed by Father D. Grasso. It says the question whether human beings can live on sidereal bodies was recently raised again "by the strange phenomenon of flying discs."

The article further stated: ". . . neither dogma nor theology would find themselves in difficulties, should science be able to ascertain the existence of human beings outside the earth."

IFSB FORMS DEPT. OF INVESTIGATION

As of March 1, 1953 a Dept. of Investigation has been formed by the IFSB to approve or disapprove of all sightings sent into the Bureau. Any person or persons that send in reports of saucer sightings will be investigated. The staff of officers is as follows: Chief Investigator, Mr. Gray Barker, Clarksburg, W.Va.; Chief Photographer, Mr. August C. Roberts, Jersey City, N.J.; Chief Aeronautics Engineer, Mr. Domonic Lucchesi, Jersey City, N.J.; Chief Astronomer, Mr. Lonzo Dove, Broadway, Virginia, and Rev. S. L. Daw, Washington, D.C. Decisions made by this Board of Investigators will be final unless proven otherwise.

TWO NEW FOREIGN REPRESENTATIVES APPOINTED

IFSB now has two new Representatives in foreign countries. They are: for France, Mr. Paul Baudat of Paris; for Australia, Mr. Edgar Jarrold of Fairfield.

Mr. Jarrold is President of the Australian Flying Saucer Bureau. He is a 34-year-old RAAF storeman.

Mr. Baudat, who is 54 years old, is a technician-electrician in signals for railways.

BBC MENTIONS IFSB AND ITS AIMS

The British Broadcasting System gave ISFB a boost by mentioning it on one of its programs, telling of its aims and its purpose. This was brought about by our British Rep., Mr. E. Plunkett.

FRANKLIN, INDIANA, TO HAVE MEMBERSHIP DRIVE—COMBINE IFSB WITH CIVILIAN DEFENSE GROUP

Again Franklin, Indiana, is first with a fine idea of getting members for IFSB. The drive is to strive for 150 to 200 members. We wish them the best of luck.

SAUCERS IN THE NEWS

UNITED STATES OF AMERICA

MEMPHIS, TENN. — Sept. 8, 1952 — A woman employee of a local newspaper said she saw a flying saucer in broad daylight. She said: "It looked like a big washtub, with a large pole through the middle. It had a light on each end of the pole, one green and one purple.

BRISTOL, CONN. — Dec. 1, 1952 — A V formation of 30 flying "objects" was seen by a Bristol woman and her neighbor. She said: "They were definitely round and wobbled from side to side as they floated by. They looked like flat ashtrays."

BRIDGEPORT, CONN.—Dec. 18, 1952—A married couple from nearby Fairfield saw two flying "saucers" over their home at an altitude of approximately 15,000 feet at 4:30 P.M. The objects were round, moved together and shot out reddish pink flames around the outer edges. Municipal airport says, "sunspots".

DALLAS, TEXAS—Jan. 6, 1953—A brilliant colored object having swept-back wings, hung in the sky for several hours, then vanished.

JAPAN—Jan. 27, 1953—United States jets chased strange clusters of red, white and green lights flying at blinding speeds through the sky. The objects remain unidentified, but were picked up by radar. In one instance, a small metallic object of disc shape, made a controlled sweeping pass at an American jet fight-bomber. It was a bright cloudless day and the pilot got a good look at the object. It was about eight inches in diameter, very thin, round and shiny.

OCEAN VIEW, VA. — Jan. 27, 1953 — A woman and her neighbor saw a big ball of fire in the sky. It was headed for a landing about a mile away. It could have been a meteor.

LOS ANGELES, CALIF.—Jan. 30, 1953— A Northrup Aircraft test pilot declares that he saw four "saucers" flying in formation near Malibu. Earlier, officials at the El Toro Marine Corps Base, southeast of Los Angeles, reported that one of their jets chased a large, fiery disc-shaped object, but was outdistanced.

CONWAY, S.C.—Jan. 29, 1953—A farmer and ex-veteran, hearing a commotion in his barn, took his gun and went out to investigate. At treetop level he noticed an object 24 feet long and 12 feet across with a light grayish color and lit up inside. The object was 8 to 10 feet deep. He said, "It was something like half-an-egg, cut from end to end." Becoming frightened, he fired his gun at the object and it flew away. Since this happened numerous livestock have died mysteriously in that area.

BRIDGEPORT, CONN.—Feb. 7, 1953 — A large undetermined explosion rocked a part of Bridgeport area on two separate days. One blast was accompanied by a flash of light. It was finally attributed to a falling meteor, although this is not yet certain.

FRANKLIN, VA.—Feb. 9, 1953—Strange circular craft about 35 to 38 feet in diameter of a silver material with windows had been hovering in the sky over Franklin for two nights. At times the objects threw off a red glow while the windows cast a bluish color. They were chased by jets, but the jets were outdistanced.

SOUTHPORT, CONN.—Feb. 23, 1953—A group of eight glowing objects which had the characteristics of flying saucers were spotted by a resident near his home. At first sight they were in a perfect box formation, remaining stationary for two minutes before they swiftly disappeared.

CHERRY POINT, N.C.—Feb. 11, 1953— The Marine Corps reported that jet planes had chased and then lost a red lighted object that flashed through the sky at astounding speed of better than 500 miles per hour.

(Continued on Page 7)

SAUCERITIS!

by John Armitage of Great Britain

The average man outwardly ridicules the fact that flying saucers exist, and generally put this phenomena down to mass hysteria, or missles propelled by wrathful housewives subject to hysterical tendencies; nevertheless, in spite of this opinion thousands of men and women from every walk of life, and from every nation, have not only seen, but have, over the last four or five years taken photographs of these mysterious objects.

A section of the Aeronautic Specialists scorn the idea that an airborne object of this shape and design can be logical, both from aerodynamic and propulsion angles—others consider that in the space of a few years these objects will become the accepted mode of air travel, and seriously consider that perhaps the U.S.S.R., utilizing the brain of abducted German Scientists, are many years ahead of the Western Powers in the field of magnetic research, producing flying discs for the purpose of obtaining vital information by photographing American defense installations, etc., at the same time testing their reliability for a more sinister role.

Another popular theory, which has support among the astronomical scientists, is that these objects come from outer space. This being the case, are our sister planets in their rarefied atmospheres capable of producing animal life as we know it in our world?

Seriously speaking, I consider the most conservative point of view must be taken because no practical proof of the existence of flying discs has ever become common knowledge. Yet the American authorities do not deny their existence and have been so obviously evasive in answering any questions produced by the press on this subject. So may we assume by this attitude, that these perhaps, if they exist, are of American origin? Nevertheless one's imagination may run riot if a study is made in this direction. One may even begin to believe that H. G. Wells had intuition when he wrote "The War of the Worlds" by the remarkable true story: On the night of August 22, 1924, our neighboring planet Mars passed within 35 million miles of this world. Observatories in the N Hemisphere were eagerly scanning the big red orb in the still, starry night hoping to catch some evidence of life, or human occupation on its surface. Every high powered radio station was silenced in the hope that some message would be flashed across space. Suddenly, after a long period of tension, first one radio station and then another picked up a distinct signal on a wave band of 6,000 meters which was recorded on film by an apparatus similar in nature to the sound recording devices used in the motion picture industry today. After these signals ceased the film was developed, and shortly after examined by a group of scientists who were astounded by what they saw. On the left hand side of the film was a series of clear and unmistakable dots and dashes (similar in nature to our Morse code and on the right hand side spaced at equal intervals a mass of jumbled lines resembling very strongly the feature of a man's face. This film was then rushed to decoding stations who after studying it for some weeks stated that they could not decode it. This film has been kept as a permanent record as proof of the historical activities on that night.

(Concluded on Page 11)

EDITORIAL

The year 1953 will be the greatest year in the world's history for spectacular displays of nature, on earth and in the heavens.

There is something unusual taking place in this vast universe. It is the time for disturbances of exceptional magnitude.

Climates and weather conditions are changing on earth. People of the northern hemisphere are experiencing weather usually associated with the southern hemisphere. Earthquakes, hurricanes, volcano eruptions, tidal waves, dust storms, etc., are reeking havoc, and will continue to do so for the rest of the year 1953.

The polar caps are building themselves up inch by inch with layers of ice and there is no sign of decreasing by thawing. If one of these polar caps should become oversized or top heavy the earth may capsize. This was believed to have happened earlier in the history of our planet Earth, which was responsible for the floods mentioned in the Bible. Proof of this was brought forth from expeditions that retraced their routes to the poles, only to find their former campsites buried under tons of ice, that had accumulated over the short span of time.

Animals have been found buried in the ice in the polar regions that were normally found in a tropical climate. These animals were perfectly preserved with grass still in their mouths where they had been grazing. Such findings only show that these animals were swept away by some great force that hit them without notice.

The time for the next capsizing may be 1953 and from all points of view, the earth is "pretty wobbly" and that time may be at hand.

Saucers from other planets have been sighted more so now than any other time in our history. The coming of the saucers may have to do with saving us from our horrible fate.

FROM THE ASSOCIATE EDITOR'S DESK

We will probably agree that some of the billions of heavenly bodies in the universe contain some form of life similar to ours on Earth. But we would probably not all agree as to when, if at all, we could expect a visit from any of these people.

I believe that it is not beyond reason to assume that some day such a visit will occur. However, I do not believe that it will happen during our lifetime. That would be too much to hope for, I think.

Our Earth, too, will eventually come to an end. But I would hate to hang by my feet until that happens!

Considering the age of our Earth, it is not unreasonable to hope that we can expect our poor planet to last another hundred billion years or so. I think we all have enough on our minds without thinking about things like that.

Published quarterly by Albert K. Bender, Editor; Max Krengel, Associate Editor; Printed by Reliable Press, Bridgeport, Conn. Subscription Price: four issues to members, $1.00; to non-members, $1.40 per year. Individual copies $.35. Exclusive publication of IFSB, P.O. Box 241, Bridgeport 2, Conn., U.S.A. Send all news and articles to this address.

LET'S LOOK AT THE MAGAZINES

LIFE MAGAZINE, Dec. 8, 1952—The World We Live In (Part One)
Feb. 9, 1953—The World We Live In (Part Two)
Excellent and should be saved.

TIME MAGAZINE, Dec. 8, 1952—Space Pioneer.

SIR MAGAZINE, January 1953—Did the Abominable Snowman Come From Mars?

MR. AMERICA, January 1953—You Are Being Watched.

FATE MAGAZINE, January 1953—The Saucer and the Monster by Gray Barker.
February 1953—I See by the Papers—Saucer shorts.

POPULAR SCIENCE, February 1953—Does Anybody Live on Mars?

MAGAZINE DIGEST, February 1953—Flying Saucers: Truth or Hoax.

COLLIERS, Feb. 28, 1953—World's First Space Suit.
March 7, 1953—More About Man's Survival in Space.

SEE MAGAZINE, March 1953—Flying Saucers the Last Word.

MALE MAGAZINE, March 1953—The Flying Saucer Heads South.

STAG MAGAZINE, April 1953—He Was Burned by a Flying Saucer.

ACTION MAGAZINE, May 1953—I Rode a Flying Saucer.

NIGHT AND DAY, March 1953—Humans Fly in the Saucers.

These magazines are in the IFSB LIBRARY as part of our collection. We will send written information to anyone that may have questions on above.

SPECIAL NOTE! The staff of Space Review wishes to inform all readers of a new page starting in our July issue. This page will be devoted to theories on the propulsion of "Flying Saucers". Contributions for this page must be received by June 10th.

ATTENTION! ALL MEMBERS! At the present time only Representatives have been granted the privilege of a free two months extension on memberships obtained for the IFSB. This privilege will now be extended to include all members. If you wish credit for any new members you must write to us and tell us the name and address of the new member you have obtained, or, the new member may inform us that you recommended him or her.

ISSUES OF SPACE REVIEW: In regards to back issues of Space Review we wish to inform all members that as our membership increases there will be less extra copies available than in the past. We still have copies of Vol. I, No. 1, on hand. All other issues are exhausted. Please do not ask for them.

STANLEY E. CROUCH, Holly Circle, Sterling, Virginia, will convert his publication, SCIENCE AND CULTURE MAGAZINE, from its mimeographed format to magnetic recording tape and wire, after one more issue.

LET'S SUBSCRIBE TO "STAR ROCKETS", the new fanzine put out by our member, Raleigh E. Multog, 7 Greenwood Road, Pikesville 8, Maryland. 12 for $1.00.

Another good fanzine, "FAN TO SEE", by our club member, Larry J. Touzinsky, 2911 Minnesota Ave., St. Louis 18, Missouri. $1.00 per year.

LET'S SNAP IT — FOR PROOF

by Reporter

August C. Roberts, New Jersey Rep.

Reading about "flying saucers", "discs", "objects", "cartwheels", "dimes", "fireballs", or anything else you want to call them is interesting, but without a photograph or other proof to back up the sightings, words are almost worthless. As yet, no one has ever really proven that "saucers" do exist, so we, as members of the IFSB, should try our best to do so. That "saucers" are real, we know, but how about proving it to the rest of the world? If we succeed, the IFSB will go down in history. When the reports start coming over the radio and appearing in newspapers close to your home town, get outside and begin looking for these flying wonders.

One of the first things to do is to get that camera out of mothballs, and have it in readiness for sudden use. As skywatchers for Civil Defense, we are in strategic positions to look for them, since CD has direct phone service from the tower to the Air Force Filter Center, and should any saucer be spotted by any other skywatch post, the Air Force will contact your post to be on the lookout for them. If witnesses are on hand when an object is sighted, the story is more likely to be believed than if only sighted by one person.

A friendly tip to assure a good photograph (if you are lucky enough to spot this phenomenon) is to practice light exposure using the moon as a guide. Most objects seem to be as bright, except their color varies from silver to bright orange, while reports even have them listed under all colors of the rainbow. Their speed, too, has been disputed as from standing motionless to thousands of miles per hour. Regardless of color or speed, aim that camera at is and press that button. If your efforts are not rewarded, do not feel too badly or give up, because the only pictures on record today have been taken this way. Perhaps you may get a clear, sharp, distinct print which will prove that there are such things as flying saucers. (See you next issue, Augie!)

NOTES OF GREAT INTEREST

The following members wish to correspond with fellow members:

Alan C. Rievman, 2634 Main Street, Bridgeport 2, Conn.

Ronald Gmyrek, Browerville, Minnesota.

Harry Calnek, Granville Ferry, Nova Scotia, Canada.

William E. Daniel, 3218 Roscoe, Dallas, Texas.

Gail Sprague, 622 S. 4th Ave., Wausau, Wisconsin.

This is your last chance to put orders in for the club emblem. Contact office, if interested, but do not send money until notified. Price is $1.00 each.

Membership fee as of January 1, 1953—$1.00 per year. Foreign $1.50.

Postage stamps are not acceptable for payment of memberships. Foreign currency will also not be accepted. Do not send personal checks.

All United States Representatives will send their monthly reports to our International Secretary: Mr. Alan C. Rievman, 2634 Main Street, Bridgeport, Connecticut.

Due to the summer vacation, the July issue of Space Review will not be out until July 15, 1953.

Send us all changes in address. Date all clippings sent in to us.

SAUCERS IN THE NEWS—Continued

OLEAN, N.Y.—Feb. 24, 1953—An object glowing and changing its color was seen in the sky. It was round in shape and changing from white to orange.

GREAT BRITAIN

DUNDRY, ENG.—Oct. 30, 1952—A mysterious flame was seen over Dundry by a number of people. It was about four feet long and lit up the sky for miles around. A huge red mass rose into the air and then burst into fragments. The Meteorological Office (Filton) said it was "lightning".

WALES—Nov. 20, 1952—A railway signalman and a police sergeant near Merthyr Tydfil saw a brilliant orange streamline object which had a disc shape speeding through the sky at 500 miles per hour.

EAST ANGLIA, ENG. — Nov. 23, 1953 — People living on the South Coast claim to have seen a strange white ball of light that had lashed across the sky illuminating their towns and villages.

LE OF WIGHT, ENG.—Dec. 15, 1952— unearthly objects seen and reported to be something like a tadpole with a flaming tail.

ANADA

MONTREAL—Oct. 28, 1952—Five flying saucers were sighted at 7:45 A.M. They were flat, shiny and traveling like jet planes, but without sound at 10,000 feet.

TORONTO—Feb. 11, 1953—The Toronto Star said today that a 1500 mile per hour flying saucer may be built in Canada. It will be about 40 feet in diameter. Blueprints of the craft have been studied by the British Air Ministry.

RAEL

HAIFI—Jan. 1, 1953—Three flying saucers were seen over Haifi flying westward over the Mediterranean at great speed.

OLAND

WARSAW—Nov., 1952—Flat, round objects were seen flying at various altitudes and speeds over Poland.

AFRICA

BULAWAYO — Jan. 15, 1953 — A professional photographer claims to have snapped a flying saucer. When the picture was examined under a powerful microscope the object appeared as a series of penciled lines of uniformed thickness, all curving the same way. Meteorological officers are baffled.

NEW ZEALAND

INVERCARGILL — Oct. 29, 1952 — Nine persons sighted a brightly colored object in the sky west of Invercargill. Some took the object to be an oval shape, and appeared to give off a red glow. There was an occasional white flash.

Objects were sighted in New Zealand at the following places on the dates given: Christchurch, Oct. 13, '52; Georgetown, Oct. 18, '52; Blenheim, Oct. 12, '52o Remuera, Sept. 14, '52; Whangarei, Sept. 28, '52; Tauranga, Sept. 9, '52; Clive, Feb. 8, '52; Herekino, Oct. 11, '52; Hobsonville, 1943; Auckland, Oct. 2, '52; Northland, Aug. 31, '52; Hamilton, Aug. 31, '52; Queenstown, Sept. 7, '52. For any details on these sightings, please contact IFSB.

AUSTRALIA

GEELONG, VICTORIA—Jan. 3, 1953—Dozens of people verify that a mysterious flare of light was seen in the sky.

BRISBANE, QUEENSLAND—Jan. 21, 1953—Two brothers claim that as they were driving their car home, a mysterious light followed them. It followed behind them, but kept up pace. It was about three feet across.

We have on record numerous sightings seen in Australia throughout 1952, supplied by our Australian Rep., Mr. Edgar Jarrold. Thanks to him!

For more detailed information on any sightings, please write to IFSB.

Let's date our clippings when sending them to IFSB.

DIRECTORY OF REPRESENTATIVES

The following names are additional since our last publication.

FRENCH REPRESENTATIVE—Paul Baudat, 7 bis rue des Acacias, Franconville, France.
AUSTRALIAN REPRESENTATIVE—Edgar R. Jarrold, 3 Ferguson Avenue, Fairfield,
    Sydney, Australia.
ALABAMA—Gene Edwards, 900 25th St., S.W., Birmingham 11.
CONNECTICUT (Newly Appointed)—Anthony Reveaux, 30 Main St., Ridgefield.
MASSACHUSETTS—Alan G. Davis, 132 Hudson Street, Northboro.
NEVADA—Blanche Dobrow, 225 Cervantes Avenue, Las Vegas.
TEXAS—William E. Daniel, 3218 Roscoe, Dallas.
UTAH—Carol McKinney, 385 North 8th East St., Provo.
    Above names will not be published again. Additional names in future issues.

OFFICERS AND COUNCIL OF THE IFSB

President: Albert K. Bender
Vice-President: Max Krengel
Secretary: Alan C. Rievman
Historian: Fred J. Bender

Dept. of Investigation

Gray Barker, *Chief*
August C. Roberts, *Photographer*
Rev. S. L. Daw, *Clergyman*
Lonzo Dove, *Astronomer*
Domonic Lucchesi, *Aeronautics*

International Council

Robert N. Webster
    Editor, Fate Magazine
Wilson "Bob" Tucker
    Author-Editor
N. Meade Layne, M.A.
    Borderland Science
    Research Associates
H. H. Fulton, President
R. J. Lavaris, Secretary
    CSI of New Zealand
Lonzo Dove
    Astronomy and Physics
Max B. Miller, President
    Flying Saucers International
Orville W. Mosher III
    Project Fan Club

International Council (Cont.)

Victor C. Johnston
    Subsurface Research Center
Elliott Rockmore
    Editor-Publisher
George D. Fawcett
    Lecturer-Sauceriana Collection
Stanley E. Crouch
    Editor-Science and Culture Magazine
Robert A. Arthur
    Editor, Author, Creator of
    Mysterious Traveler
Franklin M. Dietz, Jr.
    Editor-Publisher
Calvin Thomas Beck
    Writer
Louis H. Frahm
Jack W. Moore
    Franklin, Indiana

Space Review Staff

Editor-in-Chief..............Albert K. Bender
Associate Editor....................Max Krengel
Reporter..........................Alan C. Rievman
Reporter.................................Gray Barker
Reporter......................August C. Roberts
Foreign................................Edgar Plunkett
Foreign................................John Armitage

COMING IN JULY "SPACE REVIEW"—"THE MARS EXPLOSIONS AND FLYING SAUCERS" by Mr. Lonzo Dove (in two installments). "A NEW APPROACH TO THE SAUCER PROBLEM" by Graham F. N. Knewstub of England. A STARTLING REVELATION BY OUR PRESIDENT.

GRAY BARKER COMMENTS
by Gray Barker, Chief Investigator

The "My Theory" department in Space Review surely will be most valuable over the years, for when the opinions of many are thus aired, truth very likely will at least be touched upon. Then, one might speculate, that the truth, if and when learned, may be of such complexity that many theories so advanced may be partly in the right, but, like the blind men who went to see the elephant, all may be "in the wrong."

As for my personal beliefs, we now have ample proof of the saucers' existence, but not enough information for freezing one particular theory about what they're up to.

Lately we have had a few reports, which we must recognize as reliable, in which actual observation of saucer occupants have been made, or intelligent manipulation of such craft noted.

But with our present data considered, I believe it is important to keep an open mind on why saucers are upon us. It is important to speculate along different lines of reasoning, mentally investigating many theories which come into mind.

If one holds to pure speculation without blindly endorsing any particular view he may thus develop, he may intelligently and open-mindedly give the imagination full swing. Though it would not seem likely, the wildest theory may prove to be the most nearly true.

And after qualifying this discussion in the above manner, we might be free to ask: What if the entire structures of our religions should be shattered to bits upon the first interview with a little man who gets out of a spinning space ship.

(SEE YOU NEXT ISSUE)

THE ADAMSKI-WILLIAMSON AFFAIR
by Albert K. Bender

One of the most discussed incidents in connection with flying saucers is the Adamski-Williamson affair brought to the attention of the IFSB by our Council member, Mr. Meade Layne, M.A.

It seems that on November 24, 1952 or thereabouts a group of four persons were on a picnic lunch about ten miles east of Desert Center, Arizona. At 1:30 a large cigar-shaped object was sighted, moving eastward at great speed, or at times motionless. It disappeared, but returned in 5 or 6 minutes. A Mr. Adamski observed it with his telescope. About two hours later a saucer or disc landed about 1/4 mile distant and he took several flash exposures of it. It was about 20 feet in diameter, translucent, with a silver finish, portholes, and 3 ball bearing devices underneath. It hung about 3-4 feet off the ground. Adamski then saw some one motioning to him from a nearby elevation and he walked toward the person. The man spoke some English and also something that sounded like Chinese. He appeared to be about 23 years old, round face, tan and ruddy complexion, gray-green eyes and long sandy hair. He wore red-brown slipper-like shoes, pants tied around the ankles and a brown jacket. The visitor spoke and said that he came from another planet, came to investigate mushroom clouds seen by his people. The cigar-shaped ship was the mother ship, and that the discs came from that. He would not allow Adamski to get close to the ship. He shook hands with Adamski, and before leaving indicated that his footprints would have some significance. Mr. George Williamson made plaster casts of these footprints and they are being studied. (This whole story is being given careful study by our own IFSB before we will make any comment on its authenticity.) For further details write to us at P.O. Box 241, Bridgeport, Conn.

by Alan C. Rievman, Reporter

SAUCER SIGHTINGS BY IFSB MEMBERS

SIGHTING #7—

Rev. S. L. Daw, Rep., Washington, D.C.

Rev. Daw sighted a batshaped object coming out of a dark sky at about 5:20 p.m. on Dec. 13, 1952. It was a golden color and was visible for about 8 minutes. It was flying at a height of 1500 feet at a speed of 225 miles per hour. It was traveling north and was about 6 feet in wing span with the naked eye.

SIGHTING #8—

Mrs. Glenn C. Fuller, Member from Kentucky.

A round object was sighted at 8:30 p.m. on the night of July 30, 1952. It was a very bright white with blue around it. Its speed was about 750 m.p.h. at about 2000 feet. It was visable for a very short time, and was traveling from Northwest to Southeast with a size of about 50 feet in diameter.

SIGHTING #9—

Gilbert E. Menicicci, Rep. California.

Sighted a ball-shaped object on Nov. 2, 1952 at about 12:30 p.m., it was copper colored and it appeared to be suspended in mid-air. It was visible about one minute.

SIGHTING #10—

Anthony E. Reveaux, Rep. Connecticut.

Sighted a blip on Dec. 17, 1952 at about 4:30 p.m. while on the Ground Observing Post of Civil Defense. It was a deep golden hue and seemed to be traveling at a relatively slow speed at a height of about a mile, it was traveling in a westerly direction. There were 2 of them and their size was between 50 and 800 feet in diameter.

SIGHTING #11—

Larry Touzinsky, Member from Miss.

Sighted a sphere on Jan. 3, 1953 at about 10:30 p.m. It was red-orange and traveling south and was visible about 5 seconds.

MY THEORY by IFSB Membors

THEORY #11

Submitted by Harold F. Emridh, member from Kansas.

My theory is that the saucers are from a civilization which has outgrown wars long ago. They have seen our atomic flashes and decided that they had to investigate. I think that the saucers are to keep us imprisoned on Earth until we civilize ourselves to the point where we no longer pose a threat to them.

THEORY #12—

Submitted by Rep. Dick Campbell, Ind.

I don't think that the saucers are of earthly origin, my reason for this being that they have been sighted since 1707, and at that time, no one had any idea of guided missiles, etc. They have also sighted our atomic installations which aroused their curiosity. They are definitely from another planet.

THEORY #13—

Submitted by Gilbert E. Menicucci, Rep. California.

I believe that the saucers must be from either Venus or Mars as I agree with Professor Einstein that matter can't exist at speeds greater than light. I don't think that they are from Venus because of the great heat, little water and little oxygen in its atmosphere. Therefore, they must be from Mars.

THEORY #14—

Submitted by John Benton, Member from New York.

I think that the saucers are extra-terrestrial in origin and are unmanned. It is my opinion that they are controlled by some beings which are between the moon's orbit and us. This is the only way that the objects would be able to accelerate at the speeds that they are capable of without injuring the occupants. I believe that they'll contact us and let us know their secrets.

Theory No. 15—Submitted by Harry Calnek, Member, Nova Scotia, Canada:

I believe that the saucers are extraterrestrial and are using Mars or Venus as space stations for our planet. I think that they are propelled by anti-gravity, and I further think they have landed on Earth. They are so advanced in science that they have no fear of the people on Earth.

SAUCERITIS! — Concluded

Many famous scientists also claim to have contacted Mars by radio, among them, Senor Marconi himself and Mansfield Robinson, who in 1928 used the Rugby Transmitter for this purpose and, it is recorded, received a reply. Still, that is another story.

Can we now probe the theory that it is at least feasible to consider that the Martians have achieved the art of interplanetary travel? Anyway, it's something to think about!

ARE THEY LOOKING AT US, TOO?
by Robert A. Arthur
Editor, Author, Creator of Mysterious Traveler, International Council IFSB

My theory is that the saucers come from beyond the planetary system, and are powered either by magnetism or anti-gravity, which is probably a form of magnetism itself, and contain other world tourists, who have discovered that this planet holds intelligent life and are visiting it out of curiosity. Probably any race capable of crossing interstellar space have accomplished so much they're bored, and so tourists take trips to see earth and are becoming popular. No doubt our atmosphere and earthly conditions are unlike their own home planet so they don't land. They may be mining Venus and Mars and possibly these trips to earth are just side excursions to keep the workers from being bored. Whether they'll ever land, I don't know. I half hope they will, and half hope they won't!

EXCERPTS FROM OFFICIAL NEWS RELEASE BY
FLYING SAUCERS INTERNATIONAL
Max B. Miller, President

1. The United States Government not only knows that the saucers are real, but they also know that flying saucers are interplanetary.
2. Flying saucers either come from the planets Mars or Venus.
3. The Government will soon release information that the flying saucers are real and come from another planet!
4. Because of the recent hydrogen explosions it looks to us as if the saucers will make an undisputed appearance.
5. It is likely that a flying saucer will make its first appearance in a desert (probably in the United States).
6. The great prophet Nostradamus predicted that in late 1953: "A third world war will come to the world. A great ship from another world of higher intelligence shall land and intervene."
7. There will be a landing of a flying saucer in late 1953. This landing will be the greatest occurrence in nearly 2,000 years. It will effect nearly everything.
8. An interesting development leads us to believe, without a doubt, that flying saucers have a base on the opposite side of our moon!

(The above statements are not necessarily endorsed by the IFSB)

JOIN "PROJECT FAN CLUB" AND HELP MR. ORVILLE W. MOSHER, Director, TO GAIN ALL INFORMATION FOR HIS BOOK ON FAN CLUBS. Write to: 1728 Mayfair, Emporia, Kansas.

WE WANT YOU TO MEET

J. RONALD ALBERT, CANADIAN REPRESENTATIVE — Born at Ottawa, Ontario, on November 15, 1932. Mr. Albert is our capable Canadian Representative and lives in the Canadian capital, a city of vast beauty and great historic significance. He is a recent high school graduate and now employed by the Canadian government.

He is fortunate in having seven brothers and two sisters, all at home. His father is one of the most prominent furriers in Ottawa. It seems that this furrier has somewhat of a problem in finding one of his many sons interested in his line of work. They all seem to be interested in other things.

"Ronny" is greatly interested in sports of all kinds. He is an ardent basketball fan and travels miles to witness a game.

During the summer of 1952 he paid a visit to Bridgeport, Connecticut and his good friend, Mr. Bender, president of IFSB, Mr. Krengel, our vice-president was also pleased to meet him for the first time.

He has an excellent personality, makes quite an impression on the girls, and is a regular church-goer. His hobbies, besides sports, consists of a love for "jazz" music, science fiction, and anything supernatural.

In his "younger" days he served as counselor at Y.M.C.A. camps.

Mr. Albert has greatly increased our Canadian memberships since he has been Canadian Representative.

ASSOCIATE EDITOR

Next Issue — July 15, 1953

BRIDGEPORT 2, CONN.
POST OFFICE BOX 241
U.S.A.

Return Postage Guaranteed

To:

This issue dedicated to Miss Gail Sprague of Wausau, Wisconsin
for exceptional service to IFSB.

Space Review

Official Publication of The International Flying Saucer Bureau of U.S.A.

VOL. II, No. 3   JULY 1953   Bridgeport, Conn., U.S.A.

ENGLISH WOMAN TALKS WITH SENATOR MARCONI DURING SEANCES AND CLAIMS C-DAY EXPERIMENT WAS A SUCCESS

A Mrs. D. M. Woodall of Bristol, England, who specializes in the spiritual world claims she holds regular seances with Senator Marconi and has asked him many questions in regards to flying saucers.

IFSB conducted an experiment March 15, 1953. A message was sent to various members and officers over the world to be sent by mental telepathy at a certain time on that date. All persons that received the bulletin took part in the experiment. However, we did not know if it would be a success. We still aren't sure, however, Mrs. Woodall asked Senator Marconi this question:

Will the appeal by the IFSB be understood by the occupants of the flying saucers? Answer: YES. Other questions asked were: Where do the saucers come from? Answer: Mars. Is there life on the planet Mars? Answer: Yes. Are the saucers flown by human beings? Answer: YES. What will be the result of the appeal made by IFSB — Answer: Peace. We have many other questions and answers, but due to lack of space we must omit them, however, we will send same to anyone who may be interested.

FRENCH REPRESENTATIVE APPEARS ON RADIO PROGRAM

Paul Baudat our French Rep. appeared on a French Radio Program speaking about IFSB and the flying saucers. Questions were asked and Mr. Baudat answered them very satisfactorily. The French people are also very much interested in the flying saucers.

THOUGHT FOR THE MONTH BY GRAY BARKER

The Air Force may build a craft that will look and behave like a flying saucer. And on some far off planet some lecturer will expound: "Our operations have indeed been successful. The aborigines have imitated us most successfully, and at long last we can observe unobserved. The time for the DAY is drawing close at hand"

DIRECTOR BENDER APPOINTED UNITED STATES REPRESENTATIVE FOR TWO FOREIGN GROUPS

Our director, Mr. Albert K. Bender, has been recently named as U.S. Representative of the Civilian Saucer Investigation of New Zealand, and also U.S. Rep. for the Australian Flying Saucer Bureau. These two groups have just published their first issue of their bulletins and they are excellent and very informative.

CHANGE IN STAFF OF IFSB

IFSB now has a Director rather than a President. We have eliminated several positions on the International Staff due to better arrangement of our group. Mr. Max Krengel is still our Associate Editor and assistant to the Director.

COL. ROBERT B. EMERSON APPOINTED AS CHIEF RESEARCH CONSULTANT FOR IFSB

Col. Robert B. Emerson of Baton Rouge, La., was appointed chief research consultant by our Director June 12, 1953. Col. Emerson is the owner of the Emerson Testing Laboratories.

PEAVY PAINTING NOW AVAILABLE TO IFSB

A 5x10 reproduction of the painting, "The Eternal Supper" by Pauline Peavy, artist and philosopher, with leaflet explaining the great Valkyries (Furies, Fireballs), now called flying saucers, is now available to all members for $1.00. Mail all orders to P.O. Box 241, Bridgeport, Conn., U.S.A. This is a marvelous painting depicting the mystery of the great minds that inhabit a world of mind so vast that it is eternity in ever unfoldment of life's inner-outer atomic mystery of being.

Special article by Frank Scully in October 1953 issue

SAUCERS IN THE NEWS

UNITED STATES OF AMERICA

SAN FRANCISCO, CALIFORNIA — Feb. 14, 1953 — A Berkeley citizen saw a mysterious light streaking over the Berkeley Hills. The light hovered in the sky. It suddenly took off at a high speed and disappeared.

BURLINGTON, IOWA — Feb. 28, 1953 — Twenty persons saw a mysterious red object linger over this city for about 45 minutes. The object was described as a red ball of fire.

RUSSELLVILLE, KENTUCKY — March 2, 1953 — A bright round silver or tin-plate object was seen in the sky moving toward Bowling Green, Kentucky.

YUMA, ARIZONA — March 10, 1953 — Several officers at a gunnery meet saw what looked like flying saucers hovering over the Air Defense Command. Captain Hiaring said: "It looks like someone from another planet is spying on our gunnery meet."

BIRMINGHAM, ALABAMA — March 20, 1953 — A resident of Bessemer reported seeing 15 or 16 lights flying very low and blinking on and off.

SAN DIEGO, CALIFORNIA—May 22, 1953 — A terrific explosion from the air at 9:45 a.m. shook the city of San Diego. It broke many windows, knocked down several persons and shook houses like a heavy earthquake. It was attributed to a jet plane breaking the sound barrier.

NORWALK, CONN. — May 25, 1953 — Three Norwalk policemen saw an unidentified object at about 4 a.m. The object appeared to be moving in spurts and emitted an intense blue light. At one point it seemed like it was stalling and then rose suddenly and disappeared.

GERMANY

BERLIN — April 27, 1953 — Herr George Klein, wartime aviation advisor to Hitler, today claimed that Germany experimented with the first flying saucer shaped plane just before the war ended.

GREAT BRITAIN

LONDON, ENGLAND — March 11, 1953— The British Medical publication says that detergents have caused some flying saucer stories in America.

MONMOUTHSHIRE, ENGLAND — May 21, 1953 — A brilliant object like a globe was seen by night workers. It was hovering in the sky, sending out bright rays and lighting up a wide area early in the morning. It descended to about 8,000 feet, remained stationary for some time and then it disappeared.

NEW ZEALAND

HAMILTON, N.Z. — April 4, 1953 — A woman claims to have seen a big ball, like a moon and about the same size, yellow in the middle and glowing red at the rim. The object was sighted at about 10:45 p.m.

FAIRFIELD, N.Z. — April 5, 1953 — A light was seen in the sky that resembled a meteor or lighted lantern which dropped to the horizon.

ONGAONGA, N.Z. — April 16, 1953 — A fine thread like substance was found falling from the sky. They found it hanging on telegraph wires and on fences and spread on lawns in widely separated parts of the district.

AUSTRALIA

MELBOURNE — May 18, 1953 — A mysterious light lit up Essendon airdrome early this morning. The light lit up the whole area and was bright enough to read a newspaper by. The object was very high and traveling very fast.

ADELAIDE, S.A. — March 6, 1953 — Two railway men claim that a flying saucer whizzed over the township of Quorn, 250 miles from Adelaide, at terrific speed.

YUGOSLAVIA

BELGRADE — February 16, 1953 — Flying saucers whirled over the roofs of a district of Belgrade at varying speeds and heights.

(Continued on Page 4)

THE MARS EXPLOSIONS AND THE FLYING SAUCERS
by Lonzo Dove, Chief Astronomer, IFSB.

INSTALLMENT I.

In my letters dated January 13 and 15, 1952, to the Palomar Mount and the Lowell Astronomical Observatories and the editor of the Strolling Astronomer, Journal of the Association of Lunar and Planetary Observers, I predicted that within a day of April 15 1952, coming shortly before the close approach of Mars to Earth, there would be a new arrival of flying saucer space ships from Mars to Earth, 60 days after the launching date from Mars on February 15. This period is recognizable as the astronautically calculated and most natural time-space path for a celestial body moving in an orbit to intersect the orbits of Mars and Earth.

I predicted further that the launching and arrival dates would be marked by gigantic signals across interplanetary space, like the exploding cloud observed on Mars just one Mars Synodic Period ago on January 15 to 16, 1950, which was 60 days before the reported "saucer armada" arrival over Earth on March 17 to 18, 1950, shortly before that close approach of Mars to Earth.

My predictions were chartered out in 1950 from past flying saucer dates and a number symbol was woven into the space travel calculations for basic saucer activities.

In my letters to the Strolling Astronomer, dated April 30 and August 3, I made reference to my previous letters predicting flash cloud signals on Mars and the launching and arrival of space ships by a 60 day journey from February 15 to April 15 to 16, 1952. I pointed out that the recorded abnormal clouds observed on Mars of December 8 to 9 and 27, 1951, coincided with two of the basic periods in my saucer schedule; the return from Earth to Mars and the preceding last good look over Earth in landing tests on the date of the Mars Aphelion. I also submitted a photo copy of my chart and copies of published articles in which I predicted those very dates so prominently figured in the chart. I submitted a photograph that I took on April 16, 1952 of a huge circle cloud 30 miles in diameter and 15 miles up in the sky, a double track a mile wide, with a lead off trail going northwest toward Alaska—where next morning some high vapor trails of "unknowns" caused a nationwide military special alert!

So now, after all this was said and done, the July, 1952 issue of the Strolling Astronomer comes out and on pages 99 and 100 describes "the most interesting Martian cloud of all in our records", a big double cloud of dull hue that stood 60 to 90 miles above the surface of the planet Mars on April 16, 1952, in the region Eridania, which is beside Electris where the similar cloud was observed January 15 and 16, 1950 mentioned in the same article.

We cannot logically escape the significance of the fact that this abnormal double cloud on Mars and the equally abnormal double cloud circle over Earth occurred the very same day, which is also the very day I had calculated 2 years earlier for the main arrival of flying sucers from Mars to Earth 3 weeks before the close approach of the two planets—this latter within a day of the Rio saucer photograph.

The earlier April, 1952 issue of the Strolling Astronomer, page 47 and 51, also page 56 and 57, had described the observations of December 27, 1951 as follows: "The most conspicuous cloud, brilliant and striking, on Mars", and December 8 to 9, 1951, the "Extremely brilliant flash and exploding cloud of brief duration on Mars, certainly one of the most extraordinary phenomena ever recorded by students of Mars." These two dates are on my chart, and their nature is surely important enough for interplanetary signals.

(Concluded in October, 1953 issue)

EDITORIAL

Are we the only human beings in space? The answer to this may be "no", and then again it could be "yes".

However, the extent of space and its contents are still an unknown to the greatest mind here on earth. As you stand and gaze up at the sky, the vastness of it all makes you feel like something under a microscope. Something greater, something bigger is looking down at you through a big window of the universe.

Billions of suns, some so large that our whole solar system could be placed inside with plenty of room left over, are out there in the black inky endless unknown. When one begins to wonder how far space extends and if it does have an ending, what lies beyond, one becomes dizzy with the many strange ideas that creep into our brains. It is these thoughts that make even our greatest scientists helpless because they haven't the equipment or the knowledge they would like to have to find out and answer the mystery.

It is only logical to surmise that since our earth is probably millions of years old, there are other solar systems with planets revolving about their suns exactly like ours. One of these planets must have a civilization much older and wiser than those on earth. It is without a doubt time for them to have discovered interplanetary travel, and their form of craft most certainly could be saucer-shaped.

These people may not resemble us, but when one thinks of the vastness of space, one begins to wonder if there isn't a power that created all this, and if it was God, he certainly must have made all human beings of the same pattern, the same mold was used for the castings, whether they fly about in jet planes or in flying saucers.

DIRECTORY OF REPRESENTATIVES

MAINE (Temporary)—Harry Everett Burnham, Jr., 136 Cumberland Ave., Portland, Maine. Rep. Levinsky is in the service.

MARYLAND—Raleigh E. Multog, 7 Greenwood Road, Pikesville 8, Maryland.

LET'S LOOK AT THE MAGAZINES

LIFE MAGAZINE—April 13, 1953—The World We Live In—PartIII.
    June 8, 1953—The World We Live In—Part IV.

HIS MAGAZINE—May 1953—The Saucers Are Spies from Mars.

POPULAR SCIENCE—June 1953—Islands in the Sky.

MR. MAGAZINE—July 1953—Will Russia Steal Our Space Station?

HIT MAGAZINE—July 1953—Flying Saucers Are Back.

SIR MAGAZINE—July 1953—Is Mars Trying to Contact Us?

SAUCERS IN THE NEWS—Continued

KOREA

SEOUL — April 20, 1953 — United States airmen reported seeing a strange "delta-shaped" or triangular, object about seven feet in diameter flying at 60 to 80 miles per hour over Red lines on the western front.

Published quarterly by Albert K. Bender, Editor; Max Krengel, Associate Editor; printed by Reliable Press, Bridgeport, Conn., U.S.A. Subscription price: four issues to members, $1.40; individual copies, $.40. Exclusive publication of IFSB. P.O. Box 241, Bridgeport 2, Conn., U.S.A. Send all news and articles to this address.

A NEW APPROACH TO THE SAUCER PROBLEM

by Graham F. N. Knowstub, A.M. Brit. I.R.E., A. Inst. E.

The outstanding feature of the flying saucer problem is a fact that in spite of a wealth of observational detail provided by observers in every part of the world over a period of roughly five years, there are still no conclusive answers to the following fundamental questions: (1) Where do they come from? (2) Who make and fly them? (3) What are they? (4) How do they fly? (5) Why are they saucer shaped?

Every technique known to modern science, from photography and radar to jet interceptor aircraft, has been employed to try and solve the problem by direct observation but has failed. The time is now ripe for a new approach to the problem, an approach based upon the point of view of the designer of a flying saucer. To start with, the unique shape of these craft obviously has some vital bearing on either the principal of flight or the means of propulsion, and an analysis of the dynamics of flying discs is a reasonble starting point.

The flying disc is no new invention! The ancient Greeks knew of it centuries before the Christian era in the form of the discus. Owing to its aerodynamic properties it was a tricky thing to throw effectively, which is no doubt why it has retained its place in Olympic athletics to this day.

Basically, a discus is a wheel, and its motion is that of rolling. A driven wheel, such as the rear wheel of an automobile, is acted upon by two forces; a torque applied by the axle and friction acting at a point on the perimeter in the direction of motion and opposing the torque. In the case of the front wheels of an automobile to which no power is applied, the torque is replaced by a horizontal force acting through the center. Friction is essential to the rolling motion in both cases; without it the driven wheel would rotate without moving forward and the free wheel would slide forward without rotating. The discus is the counterpart of the free wheel, for the thrower imparts a linear motion through the center and also a rotary motion by retarding one side as the discus leaves his hand. The friction due to the air resistance during flight is greatest at the advancing edge and least at the retreating edge, and therefore is retarding the rolling motion. From this brief analysis it will be seen that there are two distinct dynamic principles of flight which are applicable to a flying disc; and which are independent of motive power or aerodynamics. The latter point indicates that the flying disc is suitable for space flight as an alternative to the rocket.

Here then is a task for the armchair scientist. A careful analysis of the reports of sightings will provide much useful material. It must be borne in mind that several totally different means of propulsion may be in use, as well as various principles of flight, and it would be wise to classify data into groups associated with specific features, such as fiery jets, vapor trails, glowing lights, etc. In this way the risk of being misled by data properly relating to a different type of craft may be reduced. At the moment we have a number of jigsaw puzzles all mixed together with a great many pieces missing; and our first task is to sort out the pieces which we have and separate the various puzzles. Work has commenced along these lines at Bristol, England, where a team of engineers and physicists are analyzing the data and investigating the physical, mechanical, and aerodynamic properties of flying discs.

HAVE WE OR HAS RUSSIA REACHED THE MOON?

by Florence Kalan, Member from California

I am not an authority on flying saucers. I have never been burned by one; taken for a ride; nor have I ever tried to shoot one down with my trusty 45—so help me!

To quote the late Will Rogers: "All I know is what I read in the newspapers."

From material gathered I concoct my own particular brand of "stew". I hope that this "pot" is seasoned to taste.

In May of 1952, scientists reported seeing a two-mile glassy tunnel on the moon (of course, it was created by natural causes, their usual solution). Bless those nature boys! Later in April 1953, reports of black darts shooting out from the moon were presumed to be rockets. Personally, I consider rockets an obsolete device to our extraterrestrial neighbors. I assume that they in their small craft are brought to the upper regions of our atmosphere in huge mother ships, then released to point of destination.

Suppose the scientists miscalculated and the tunnel was created by beings of our earth variety. Old man Moon hasn t been smiling at us just to perpetuate the good neighbor policy. There is something going on behind the old man's back and he's not talking! The most powerful eye in the world at Mount Palomar cannot see through the old boy.

Reliable sources contend there are two mysteries in our skies. Have we or has Russia reached the moon! If we haven't, it wouldn't be the first time we have been fooled.

SPOTLIGHT ON AUSTRALIA

by Edgar R. Jarrold, President, Australian Flying Saucer Bureau

Like IFSB, we are engaged in serious research into the many problems associated with flying saucers, and like other similar organizations we are working strenuously towards obtaining the ultimate solutions of where saucers come from, why, etc. We have great faith in the determined efforts of IFSB; we have global sightings in our files dating from 1661 onwards, Lunar, Martian, and Venusian phenomena.

We enjoy official exchanges of theories and sightings and are looking forward to even greater efforts in the future. Particularly, we genuinely appreciate the wonderful help given us, so unselfishly, by IFSB. We are proud, too, that our efforts are aimed at continued, even closer cooperation with the world's major investigation body, for only in universal unity do we see hopes of a quick solution.

Currently we believe from recorded data, that Mars is some way connected with the saucers' origin and we are exploring statistics suggesting that saucer reports occur in two year cycles. Previous heavy years, 1950 and 1952, coincided with Martian approaches. We anticipate even greater sightings in 1954 and 1956 when Mars comes even closer to earth. The years 1953 and 1955 should be fairly light ones and we hope to add more portions to the extra-terrestrial picture slowly unfolding. We take our task seriously and forsee increased public attention in the near future leading to more research, and we are proud of our vigorous association with IFSB. We send greetings to all.

"FANTASY VERSUS LOGIC"

by Dominick C. Lucchesi, Chief Aeronautics Engineer Serving the IFSB

For some time, it has been my intention to elucidate on the subject of discs, saucers, and other phenomena which have been observed in flight through our atmosphere. Many qualified persons have seen them and pondered the same question as, what are the discs; how do they propel themselves; and what type of beings guide them? I herewith state that the discs, their occupants, and their propulsive force are entirely within the reach of the research divisions of some of our larger aeronautical corporations. All other theories as of; beings from outer space; magneto-gravatic drives; and other ridiculous assumptions; are nothing more than illusions created by the fervid and over-active imagination of too many science-fiction fans who have allowed their enthusiasm to overcome their logical approach to a problem of this sort.

With common sense and forethought, it is easy to visualize the construction of a navigable disc which will perform as described by our more dependable observers. With enough thought given to this matter, it is easy to see that the greatest accomplishment achieved by the makers of said discs is the obscurity surrounding their origin. The claims of the ridiculous, fantastic speeds attained by the discs are claims and nothing more. As there is no concrete evidence to substantiate these unusual high velocities, I claim that the maximum speed attainable by an object of this type in our atmosphere lies in the vicinity of 1800 to 2000 miles per hour. However, this is not due to inherent drive energy, but instead by the destructive heat brought about by unavoidable skin friction at speeds higher than the above named. This does not apply to travel in outer space, where speeds in excess of 3 miles per second are entirely possible.

Actually, a great number of fans arrive at an assumption without ever having observed a disc, which to me is not the proper way to deduce their origin; when a reference to an advanced engineering library would definitely prove more enlightening as to their source. In my contemplation of the mental processes of the average science-fiction fan, I have come to the conclusion that their attitude is, "We know so little fact, therefore, why not assume the exalted attitude of knowing what they are, for few will dispute our claims".

I hereby claim, that within my possession rests the complete technical data necessary to construct a vehicle that would fulfill all requirements, and more, than are claimed by said saucer observers, such as; take off in any attitude or direction; the ability to change course instantaneously such as climb, dive, and right angle turns; and would also incorporate, though not entirely necessary, a rotating outer rim. The drawing of this object, now nearing completion, will soon be submitted to our director, Mr. Albert K. Bender.

Hoping this will not deter my fellow science-fiction fans from exercising their wonderful imaginations, I remain your humble servant.

NEXT MONTH: This page will be entitled THEORIES ON PROPULSION, edited by Mr. Dominick C. Lucchesi. Members are asked to send in their theories for publication.

In our October issue you will read "SPEAKING OF SAUCERS" by Judith Gee, "FLYING SAUCERS—WHAT AND WHY?" by Hugh Peard, a short story by Bob Tucker entitled "EYES THAT WATCH", plus other interesting items.

WITNESSING THE UNKNOWN

by Reporter, August C. Roberts, New Jersey Rep.

The Director of the IFSB has requested me to describe to the readers of SPACE REVIEW just how it feels to see a saucer exactly as I did on July 28, 1952. My first impression was one of amazement, since the Air Force disbelieves their existence. My mind reacted like this; I wanted to believe that our government and Air Force might be right and that the people were seeing things that were non-existant, but here was the exact proof before me.

I was serving as a ground observer on routine duty with a 9x30 power binoculars in my hand. The binoculars were focused on the saucer going through its movements. I noted the round shape which was unlike anything else I had ever seen before. The color of this object fascinated me because it was an eerie orange with a reddish brown rim. There was a dot in the center of the same color. When the object spun this center changed to the same glowing red as the rim and could be seen quite clearly. At this point it began to speed up; the whole thing flickered and pulsed sitting on its edge in the sky. It had considerable depth. About the best way to describe this, is to visualize two half dollars held together at arms length and turned slightly to see the edge. The rim appeared to be as thick as the edge was wide. The whole thing was flat and resembled identically the two half dollars. It was somewhere between fifty to one hundred feet in diameter.

While watching it I had that odd feeling in the pit of my stomach, and thought to myself, here is something everyone is searching for and I have a box seat. I had seen many planes while serving as a spotter for Civil Defense and the army, but this machine certainly beat them all. It made no sound and looked powerful and deadly, although it appeared to be just observing. I began to think to myself that it could belong to our Air Force, but I just cannot bring myself to feel that any country on earth has advanced that far to construct such a fabulous machine. It looked like something out of another world and I have always believed the so-called flying saucer comes from some far away place. If you had witnessed exactly what I had, I'm sure that you would believe it came from far out of space.

NOTES OF INTEREST

SPECIAL NOTICE: Copies of August C. Roberts' flying saucer photographs may now be purchased from IFSB for $1.00 per copy. Address all orders to P.O. Box 241, Bridgeport, Conn., enclosing postal money order.

REQUEST FOR CORRESPONDENCE: Edward Fournier, Jr., 24 Main Street, Bradford, Rhode Island, U.S.A., wishes to correspond with members from all foreign countries.

LAPEL EMBLEMS: This is the last chance to get a club emblem. All persons still interested please contact us as soon as possible but do not send the $1.00 fee until notified.

COMING SOON: "NEW FRONTIERS" by Desmond Leslie, a book about the flying saucers. Mr. Leslie is a member of IFSB.

READ TERRA: This is a fanzine by Gilbert E. Menicucci, our California representative.

JOIN THE FLYING SAUCER CLUB: 42 Rothbury Road, Hove 3, Sussex, England.

PRE 1900 SAUCER SIGHTINGS

Submitted by Donald G. Wiggins, Member from Mass.

March 22, 1880—Kettenau, Germany—Several brilliantly luminous objects were sighted just before sunrise. They were described as rising from the horizon and moving from east to west.

March 19, 1887—Two strange objects fell into the sea near a Dutch barkentine. As described by the skipper, C. D. Sweet, one of the objects was dark and the other brightly luminous. The glowing object fell with a loud roaring sound. The ship's master was sure it was not a meteor.

January 25, 1878—Denison, Texas—A farmer who lived some six miles south of the city sighted a peculiar object in the sky about the size of an orange which continued to grow in size. When it was directly over him it was about the size of a large saucer and at a great height.

May 4, 1888—New Zealand—An oval shaped disc was reported speeding high overhead.

August 26, 1894—A British Admiral reported sighting a large disc with a projection like a tail. A year after this both England and Scotland buzzed with stories of triangular shaped objects seen in the skies. Most astronomers, at that time, believed the objects had come from outer space. Planes and dirigibles were unknown at that time.

April 9, 1897—Midwestern United States—Flying at a great height a huge cigar shaped device was seen with short wings projects from the sides of the object. For almost a week the aerial visitor was sighted around the midwest as far south as St. Louis, and as far west as Colorado. Several times red, green, and white lights were seen to flash in the sky; some thought the crew of the strange craft might be trying to signal the earth.

April 16, 1897—The thing, whatever it was, disappeared from the midwest. But on April 19 the same object, or a similar one, appeared over West Virginia. Early that morning the town of Sisterville was awakened by blasts of the sawmill whistle. Those who went outside their homes saw a strange sight. From a torpedo shaped craft overhead, dazzling searchlights were pointing downward, sweeping the countryside. The thing appeared to be about 200 feet long, some 30 feet in diameter, with stubby wings and red and green lights along the sides. For almost 10 minutes the aerial visitor circled the town, then swung eastward and vanished.

NEXT MONTH: SIGHTINGS FROM 1900 TO 1947

MORE ABOUT THE ADAMSKI-WILLIAMSON AFFAIR

Following is an excerpt from a letter received by our director from Professor George Adamski:

"In the first place, there were seven of us present. Second, Desert Center is not in Arizona, it is in California. Third, there was no two-hour interval. Fourth, I did touch the ship, and when my book comes out it reveals all of this word by word, step by step."

The director wishes to state that any erroneous statements regarding this affair in the April, 1953 issue were due to misinformation supplied to the Bureau. Our director will notify members when Prof. Adamski's book is ready. Then you may form your own opinions.

SIGHTINGS
by IFSB Members

by Alan C. Rievman

SIGHTING #12—

F. Douglass Ackman, M.D., Member from Canada.

Sighted a bluish green object flying very low at a speed of about 1000 mph. There was no exhaust present, and it was completely silent. It was sighted by Dr. Ackman with about a dozen relatives on the night of August 16, 1950 at 7:55 p.m.

SIGHTING #13—

Rev. S. L. Daw, Rep. Washington, D.C.

A white, fiery diamond shaped object was sighted on the night of January 16, 1953 from 10:35 to 10:45 and then from 10:55 to 11:25 p.m. over the Potomac River. It was traveling from SW to NE and at a very high speed at about 3000 ft.

Members are asked to send in their sightings for publication or for investigation.

Report Strange Object Landed in Grand Canyon — Looked Like Parachute.

May 30, 1953 — A parachute dropped into the Grand Canyon out of nowhere. No planes were heard overhead, and a helicopter was sent into the Canyon to investigate. Later, the helicopter was unable to negotiate the currents in the Canyon and a Navy expert had been sent for, to see what the mysterious, white, round object might be, that is lying on the floor of the Canyon. Submitted to IFSB by Member Joe Barbieri of West Haven, Conn.

Frank Scully Now Member of International Council

Mr. Frank Scully, author of "Behind the Flying Saucers", is now a member of the International Council of IFSB. Despite the fact that True Magazine did not go along with the book written by Mr. Scully, IFSB feels that the book did contain much valuable information of interest to our organization. We are sure that you will enjoy his article in October Space Review.

THEORIES
by IFSB Members

THEORY #16—

Submitted by Rep. Paul Baudat of France.

I believe that the saucers exist because I don't think all people that have seen them could be victims of hallucination. I also believe that they are from some other heavenly body for two reasons: (1) If they were of Earth origin the secret could not have kept this long. (2) There is no reason for us to say that we are the only living beings in the whole Universe.

THEORY #17—

Submitted by Orville W. Mosher of the International Council, IFSB.

In my opinion the saucers are space ships operated by beings from another world, who would like to make contact with us, but are afraid to do so after seeing us. However, I think that some day they will land.

THEORY #18—

Submitted by Anthony E. Reveaux of Connecticut, Rep.

My theory is that the saucers are using a power source so great in magnitude that it is beyond our comprehension, probably cosmic rays or some other unknown ray, or it might be a space-warp which would account for the various colors and shapes, maneuverability and the speeds which have been reported.

THEORY #19—

Submitted by Pauline Peavy of the International Council, IFSB.

It is evident that the saucers are from Mars, just as we are. Every atom in our being has its own milky way, its own central sun or nucleus, its spiral nebulæs; yet we are atoms so poorly conceived that we disintegrate into ASH, that terrible pit of abandon when our seed is too rotten to return to its matrix or wombing form.

THEORY #20—

Submitted by Ronald Kinnear, Rep. New York.

My theory on the miniature saucers that have been sighted is that they are scout ships controlled from a mother ship which is lying outside the atmosphere. These small discs probably have some way of recording things, perhaps by TV.

NEWS FROM GREAT BRITAIN
by Captain E. L. Plunkett, British Rep., IFSB

For the benefit of new members both at home and overseas, the IFSB first became known in this country due to a small paragraph which appeared in a well known London newspaper during August, 1952. This led to an interchange of correspondence between myself and its founder, the outcome of which culminated in my being made the sole British representative of IFSB.

The British branch was formed on September 19, 1952 from which my nomination dates. Bristol newspapers were extremely interested and cooperative and this resulted in five writeups being given at various times, all of which were excellent, inas much that the flying saucer phenomena was not made the subject of ridicule.

The London daily (which had incidentally started the ball rolling), followed with a small paragraph stating my appointment, and the result was that letters started arriving from points as far apart as Germany and New Zealand.

Meanwhile, an Episcope had become available, which led to talks being given to social clubs, Rotary, astronomical groups, etc. In several cases members formed a "brainstrust" following the illustrated talks, and some interesting questions were asked and answered.

The type of member attracted to date has been extremely gratifying, in that they have been culled from the aeronautical and professional fields, which include electronic experts, radar personnel, ex-officers of the armed services, amateur astronomers, etc.

It has been, and still is, our avowed intention to commence work on a model saucer, but due mainly to the lack of a suitable work shop and equipment this has not yet become possible.

British members are requested to send all articles for insertion in future issues of SPACE REVIEW in ample time prior to its publication each January, April, July, and October yearly. Send copies to me 6 weeks before each issue for onward transmission to HO. All members are invited to contribute items.

Recently, a Mr. Richard Hughes who, unbeknowingly set up the "Flying Saucer Club" in Sussex, was greatly surprised to hear of our organization. We have mutually become members of each others organizations.

The members of the British Branch of IFSB send their best wishes to all members over the world.

A REVIEW: AERIAL PHENOMENA RESEARCH ORGANIZATION

APRO began officially June, 1952 when the constitution and by-laws were drafted and approved. There are 42 full term members in APRO. They do not strive for a high membership count. They collect and track down sightings, attempting by investigation to eliminate hoaxes, misconceptions of conventional objects, balloons, etc. APRO is non-profit and publishes a bulletin with information compiled by the headquarters members from reports sent in by members. The constitution has an Anti-Communist clause for obvious reasons. Membership dues are $3.50 per year. The director of APRO is Mrs. Coral E. Lorenzen, a former newspaper writer. She has lectured on saucers for the air-force at the Greenbay filter center.

The APRO bulletin, which is mimeographed, gives a detailed description of recent saucer reports, and articles generally concerning saucers. One of the improvements which could be made is the stapling together of the issues for more convenience. The printing of the bulletin is very legible. However, I feel that too much unimportant detail is given in their sighting reports.

Overall, APRO is doing a commendable job in attempting to solve the saucer mystery.

ASSOCIATE EDITOR

NEXT ISSUE: A REVIEW OF THE AUSTRALIAN FLYING SAUCER BUREAU

WE WANT YOU TO MEET

PAUL BAUDAT, FRENCH REPRESENTATIVE, IFSB — Our French representative was born at Lausanne, Switzerland on August 29, 1898. He has three brothers, one of whom lives in Seattle, Washington, another lives in France, and the third lives in Switzerland.

After having studied to become a professor, he had to interrupt his studies due to bad health. He then branched into the electrical industry which interested him most. Having come to Paris when he was 20, in order to make a thorough investigation of electricity, he launched into the installations of lights, motors, telephone, and motor cars in private homes and large industrial plants.

Since 1926 he has been working for the Paris Railway Signal Company where he is now at the head of the Equipment and Upkeep department of the switching and signalling railway stations. Before this he was head of the Upkeep department of signals for the Underground Metropolitan Railway of Paris.

He married in 1923. He has a daughter of 25 named Paulette, employee of the P.T.T. He has two granddaughters, Michelle and Claudine. His hobby is gardening since he has always lived in the suburbs of Paris. He likes wireless, camping, and more recently, flying saucers.

ASSOCIATE EDITOR

(Next issue out October 15, 1953)

COMING IN FUTURE ISSUES:

Articles by David Baxter of England; Pauline Peavy; Frank Scully; and many others.

POST OFFICE BOX 241
BRIDGEPORT 2, CONN.
U.S.A.

Return Postage Guaranteed

To:

This issue dedicated to August C. Roberts of Jersey City, New Jersey
for exceptional service to IFSB.

Space Review

Official Publication of the International Flying Saucer Bureau

VOL. II, No. 4   OCTOBER 1953   Bridgeport, Conn., U.S.A.

THE FIREBALL INCIDENT IN NEW HAVEN, CONN.

On August 22, 1953, Mr. August C. Roberts, a member of the Department of Investigation of IFSB, paid a visit to a group of saucer people in New Haven known as S.P.A.C.E. From a Mr. Joseph Barbieri he learned that a strange explosion had occurred on August 20, 1953. The time was after 9:00 p.m. The ball of fire that was sighted left a gaping hole in a large Omelia signboard made of 20 gauge steel.

Mr. Barbieri and Mr. Roberts went out to have a look at the sign, and also see if any evidence could be found as to what caused the incident. They found a fairly large hole at least a foot square, and the metal was ripped and curled due to the terrific impact.

One local resident who lives about two hundred feet away, told them that she saw from her window, a streak of light go by, and almost immediately heard a loud explosion that shook the house, and at the same time, she said, the house lights dimmed.

When she and others went out to investigate they saw smoke pouring from a hole in the sign, and a smell like that of rotten eggs. Police and firemen arrived quickly, and a large crowd gathered.

It was learned that a man driving a car just about to pass the sign, saw a red ball of fire about six inches in diameter trailing a tail, leave the sign, and pass in front of his auto about thirty feet away. It tore thru the top of a large tree, just missing telephone and power lines, and disappeared at a very high speed in the direction of East Rock.

Upon examining the sign rather closely Mr. Roberts found no evidence of fire, nor were there any marks of powder burns. But, imbedded in the metal were foreign elements. With a pair of pliers Mr. Roberts took some pieces of the sign and brought them to IFSB headquarters. They were sent for analysis by our Director, Mr. Bender.

LATE BULLETIN

A source, which the IFSB considers very reliable, has informed us that the investigation of the flying saucer mystery and solution is approaching its final stages.

This same source to whom we had referred data, which had come into our possession, suggested that it was not the proper method and time to publish this data in Space Review.

ANSWER TO NUMEROUS INQUIRIES

The IFSB is puzzled and somewhat surprised by the numerous inquiries it has received regarding the same subject. The writers all desire to know what information we had available on persons having actually been taken for a ride in flying saucers.

Since we cannot answer all the inquiries we received, we are giving our answer now: To the best of our knowledge no such incident has ever taken place.

AUSTRALIAN FLYING SAUCER MAGAZINE

The IFSB fully recommends the magazine put out by the AFSB. It is one of the best in the field, and the information it contains is true and to the point.

STATEMENT OF IMPORTANCE

"The mystery of the flying saucers is no longer a mystery. The source is already known, but any information about this is being withheld by orders from a higher source. We would like to print the full story in Space Review, but because of the nature of the information we are sorry that we have been advised in the negative."

We advise those engaged in saucer work to please be very cautious.

EDITORIAL

When you read the newspaper today you very seldom see anything about Science on the front page. Usually science gets a small inconspicuous spot on the last page or thereabouts.

Yet such things as the number of Atom bombs Russia has in her stock pile and the number of H-Bombs United States has hidden away appear on the front page. The people of the world do not realize it, but just reading that little bit will make you wonder, just what will all this end up with and what lies ahead in the future. The powers of the world are building themselves up for the worst holocaust this Earth has ever seen, and the destruction that is wrought will be so great that men will be back where they started in the caves. As is said in the word of God, "fire and brimstone will be the end".

The building of stockpiles of such deadly weapons can lead to but one goal, and that is too horrible to even contemplate.

Sit down and figure all of the money that has been spent on these bombs, and you will find that it would add up into figures that you and I could not even write. If only all of this money had been put to a more intelligent use, we would today be on the moon and even on Mars. Our cities would be something out of a dream book, with modern and scientific devices that would make life something worthwhile. Cures for cancer, and the dreaded diseases would not be a mystery, but an actuality. Interplanetary travel would today be with us in all of its glory, while visits from other worlds would be an everyday occurrence. Scientists of today have the necessary knowledge to go ahead with space travel, but they lack the money to push such a project.

If only the peoples of the world would forget about self-destruction and concentrate on building a better world, there would be work for everyone and no time to think about harming our next door neighbor.

The men in the saucers are much wiser than we think, why should they destroy us, when we will no doubt do it ourselves.

MAY I TAKE THIS OPPORTUNITY IN SAYING FAREWELL TO ALL MEMBERS AND OFFICERS. THANK YOU FOR ALL THE HELP AND KIND DEEDS YOU HAVE GIVEN IFSB.—*The Director.*

A SPECIAL REVIEW:

"THE FLYING SAUCERS HAVE LANDED" by Desmond Leslie and George Adamski. Publication date, October 23, 1953. Price $3.50. British Book Centre, 122 East 55th St., New York 22, N.Y., or at your local book stores. Illustrated.

"The Flying Saucers Have Landed" is in our estimation a fine book and we recommend it to all of our members and officers.

The first part of the book deals with sightings dating from 1290 A.D. and is an excellent record of pre-1947 sightings for all members to have in their files. Mr. Desmond Leslie has done the job that IFSB has long hoped someone would attempt. Having these sightings printed in book form saves the Saucer Organizations much time in searching through their files for data on a particular incident they may want information about.

The second part of the book by George Adamski is on the fantastic side, but it is for the readers to judge and make comment. Mr. Adamski claims to have made actual contact with a saucer-man, who used mental telepathy for communication. He also states that the man claimed he was from Venus and that all planets in our solar system are inhabited. There are actual photographs of the cigar shaped objects and also of the saucers themselves that Mr. Adamski took with his camera. There is a drawing of the creature he is supposed to have met.

FOOTNOTE TO FLYING SAUCERS

by Frank Scully—author of "Behind the Flying Saucers."

Three years ago I seemed to act as umpire between the Saucerians and the Pentagonians and published my findings in a book that has since gone around the world. At least it has been published in ten languages and may even have been published behind the Iron Curtain, for all I know.

My findings seemed to have poked holes in the Pentagonian position that believers in flying saucers were either (a) screwballs or (b) perpetrators of hoaxes. I left the Air Force with 34 sightings that had left them mystified.

I sat in on a briefing of Air Force Reserve officers the other day and found that the Air Force position had changed greatly since that 1949 report of their project saucer. They no longer think believers are victims of mass hysteria. They happen now to have 750 sightings which have them stumped and most of these were reported by their own technicians and were caught on their own radar scopes. In other words, they are a good deal nearer today the position I advanced in "Behind the Flying Saucers" in 1950.

Meanwhile the front-runners for the earlier Pentagonian line are left holding a fairly empty bag. Flying saucers remain a most controversial subject and those who ridicule what others see are well within their rights, but they must stick to the subject and not throw mud on the private character of those who believe that these objects are not light reflections, mirages, or automobile hub caps.

For myself, I believe that flying saucers, like girls, are here to stay. What they are doing may remain a mystery for a while but their presence in our atmosphere is longer open to doubt. I suspect that they are mapping our magnetic patterns and studying particularly our magnetic fault zones.

Our earlier position that these space ships were magnetically propelled has not been assailed. That some of their ships grounded (not crashed) and could not take off again, would certainly make them wary of landing again until they were quite sure that magnetic conditions would make those take-offs no longer subject to chance.

This requires a vast knowledge of the magnetic conditions of the universe. The visitors from space are in all probability several light years ahead of us in such knowledge and we are only getting an inkling of what such a force is and how it operates on this earth, which is, after all, nothing but a huge dynamo traveling in three directions at the same time, for it spins, follows an orbit, and wobbles all at once.

Before I complete my next book on this vast and mysterious subject, I hope to have the answers to much of this mystery. Meanwhile it is comforting to know that the Air Force has moved over much closer to our original position and that I need no longer feel grounded among the flying saucers, but can take off from where I left off. I hope I don't shock the critics as badly the second time as I did the first.

"THE SAUCERIAN"—Fact—Fiction—Philosophy about the Flying Saucers. Published bi-monthly at 35 cents per copy or 6 issues $1.50. Edited and published by Gray Barker, Box 981, Clarksburg, West Virginia. A few copies of first issue containing West Virginia "Monster" Story are still available.

"Who Keeps His Head in the Stars and His Feet on the Ground"—*Gray Barker.*

THE MARS EXPLOSIONS AND THE FLYING SAUCERS
by Lonzo Dove, Chief Astronomer IFSB

Installment II

The fine book, "The Planet Mars", by G. deVaucouleurs, published in London in 1950, says that "Mars remains the only planet whose phenomena cannot be easily interpreted by the sole use of the physical and chemical laws applied to inorganic matter."

The clouds on Mars, their correspondence with astronomical aspects and space travel plans between Mars and Earth, are shown to be artificial from every angle of reasoning, and not caused by non-biological natural events on a planet like Mars. The saucer activities on Earth explain the synchronous Explosions on Mars, while the Mars events explain the origin of the flying saucers. The evidences thus accumulating cannot be ignored much longer.

Of all the scientific thinkers, students of astronomy with its inherent mind-expanding quality of the vastness of space and time and numbers of world evolutionary possibilities, should be the last to suffer the blighting effect of commercializing which brands as unprofitable the adventurous love of science for the sake of pure science itself.

It is not at all in the scientific spirit for organized groups of scientists to adopt the obscurantist policies of bigotry which held back science during the dark ages, and to dictate against free discussion of observations, just because it may be contrary to popular belief and may irritate some prejudice.

How in the name of science can a "noted" scientist publish that there is "zero chance" for space ships to be coming from a neighbor planet? Or after admitting to uncertainty and ignorance about radar detection, then to declare dogmatically that "in the opinion of experts it cannot and does not see flying saucers". How can they know this, since this is the very point of admitted uncertainty? This is on a par with another self-contradiction, "invisible clouds that reflect light", posed as the "cause of flying saucers". (Science Service releases: Science News Letter of August 30, 16, and 9, 1952).

Forgetful of the astro-physical fact that any intelligence on Mars arose a billion years ago at the peak of evolutions on that less-massive planet, and would have used their intelligence to invent artificial means of survival through the withering of their planet to the present day, and could be coming across space in the amazing flying disks.

From the way some professors of science go out of their way to explain away the saucer phenomena, we might conclude that they have something to hide. The trouble is, we the people do the observing of evidences, while those who never have seen a flying saucer make a show by denying the existence of such things. How stupid do they think we are?

Let us not thus discredit the names of "science" by immature statements of more emphasis and less sense than the fanaticism of religion. Let us not conduct a scientific laboratory determination upon observations by declaring beforehand what the answer must not be. True science seeks the truth whatever and wherever it may be.

SPEAKING OF FLYING SAUCERS
by Judith L. Gee, News Reporter, London

I know nothing at all about "flying saucers"! I only know what I read in the papers, which is precious little. But ignorance has never yet stopped any human from talking, or speculating, and in this manner we reveal our lack of knowledge, our pig-headedness, or our desire to be enlightened.

I accept that the flying saucers are not spots before the eyes, hoaxes, reflections, etc.

They may be visitors from space. Having spoken about the man from Mars for so long, we may have conjured him out of nowhere into here! Wonders will never cease, so why not this too?

If flying saucers come from beyond the earth's sphere, it is possible that they operate in a different octave of sense to us. Our bodies and minds impose definite limits upon our vision, hearing, speach, touch and taste. Imagine the difficulty of communicating with an entity who has another octave of sense impressions. Time may have a different meaning. The day-night sequence of our earth may seem year long to them, or flash by in a second. (I use time terms as relative to our conception and usage).

Yet sages, throughout history, have tried to impress upon us how very narrow and limited our time range is. Reports speak constantly of the immense speed and swift appearance of flying saucers, and the ability to make abrupt turns which would disrupt an earth machine and black-out a human pilot.

This suggests that "they" have different bodies than ourselves, and it is possible that "they" operate on a different frequency of vibration. On a higher pitch, as it were.

This suggests that they may not be visible to us! Invisible men from Mars suggests a new terror from Earth beings! All I want to point out is, that when we do see them, they may flicker in our sight and come and go in our vision in a manner we are not prepared for, from our own solidflesh.

Their dimensions of height, breadth, depth and duration, may be different from ours. We may have to alter all our conceptions of time-space continum, which we accept as life on Earth. Such a revolution of mind is going to shake us more than wars, earthquakes and conversion to a new religion.

The very notion of it brings science and the armed services howling down the wind on our tracks. But, this is literally beyond us all. We are all here on the same Earth and liable to the same influences. If some of us get cold feet, the rest of us will maintain stout hearts.

Personally, I think this the most thrilling thing to happen in any generation, and I'm devoutly thankful to be alive, here and now, to participate in the brave new world we shall have to meet and greet.

I would like to end on the note that Charles Fort in his books prophecised that men would venture on lands beyond the skies, within our century. All flying saucer devotees will find much to think about in his books. We are living perpetually on the edge of mystery, and hug the delutions that we know it all. When, as truth claims, we know nothing at all.

SAUCERS IN THE NEWS

UNITED STATES OF AMERICA

BRUSH CREEK, CALIF.—June 20, 1953—
On June 20, 1953, two titanium miners,
John Q. Black and John Van Allen claimed
that a flying saucer landed in their mining
camp on two separate occasions, and that a
little man got out and scooped up a bucket
of water, which he handed to someone inside the ship. They reported this to the
local sheriff's office and asked if they
might fire upon the little man. They were
told not to do so, but to try and capture it
alive. Since the saucer was supposed to
have landed on May 20 and June 20, many
speculated that it would land again on
July 20, so newspaper men, photographers
and the like gathered on that day for the
return visit of the little men, but they were
all disappointed in the fact that the little
men did not show up. The little town received nationwide fame from this little
incident and from all reports they sold
more soda pop that day, than any day
known.

WASHINGTON, D.C.—July 15, 1953—Reports from Middletown, Conn., state that
what some people may be calling saucers
is a new type of aerial flare invented for
our airplanes.

SAN CLEMENTE, CALIF.—July 31, 1953—
A skipper of a fishing boat claims that two
oblong, silvery objects buzzed by his fishing craft, and for a while hovered over
his boat.

MOSCOW, IDAHO — Aug. 10, 1953 — A
mysterious "bright, flat object perhaps 200
feet in diameter", darted overhead. Jets
were sent up and searched for 45 minutes
with no results.

SAN ANTONIO, TEXAS—Aug. 27, 1953—
A ball of fire the size of a watermelon,
round, glowing, exploded sending spark
flying above the heads of several children.
It was called ball lightning by the weather
bureau.

CHESTER, NEW JERSEY—Sept. 18, 1953—
A strange object sighted over this town.
Tipped on end, long, slightly curved tail.

SEQUOIA-KINGS CANYON, NAT. PARK,
CALIF.—July 29, 1953—Weird flashes of
bright light, witnessed four times in five
days along the middle fork of the Kaweah
River, baffled park officials and visitors.
At one time a big yellow ball about 1000
feet in diameter rose from that point.

SACRAMENTO, CALIF.—July 1, 1953—A
red ball of fire sighted in the sky between
10:45 and 11 p.m., it remained in sight
for about five minutes and then exploded
and disappeared from view.

SPECIAL NOTICE TO ALL
HONORARY MEMBERS OF IFSB

All honorary member hips are hereby
suspended until further notice. If the present honorary members wish to remain on
our new mailing list they should notify us
as soon as possible.

SAUCER CONVENTION IN
LOS ANGELES

Mr. Max B. Miller, Pres. of Flying Saucers International, reported that the recent
Flying Saucer Convention held in Los Angeles on August 16, 17, and 18 was well
received. Many noted speakers were there
including Frank Scully, Jeron Criswell,
Truman Bethurum. Approximate attend-
ance was estimated at 1500. Two thousand
were turned away on Monday night when
Criswell spoke. Rep. from major radio and
TV networks came, as well as delegates
from Chicago and London.

NEW GROUP FORMED: Spheres, Inc.,
8054 Laurel Grove Ave., North Hollywood, Calif.

SUBSCRIBE TO: Interplanetary News,
care of Genevieve A. Johnston, Joshua
Tree, California.

Join Civilian Defense and Help.

A SPECIAL ANNOUNCEMENT
by IFSB

At a meeting held on September 9, 1953 at Bridgeport, Conn., the five members of the executive staff agreed upon publishing the following statement in the October 1953 issue of Space Review:

"After serious consideration of all aspects involved in the operation of the International Flying Saucer Bureau, it has been decided to completely reorganize.

"Effective January 1, 1954, we will no longer be known as the International Flying Saucer Bureau, which specialized only in the mystery of the Flying Saucers.

"All subscription to Space Review end with this issue. Provisions regarding refunds due subscribers will be found elsewhere in this issue."

COMMENTS ON THE ABOVE STATEMENT

On January 1, 1954, a new organization will come into existence with Mr. Albert K. Bender and Mr. Max Krengel as directors.

This organization, comprised of individuals, each a specialist in hi or her particular field, will confine itself to matters pertaining to the universe in general and will be mostly technical in nature.

There will be no paid memberships in this group available. Memberships will be restricted to the specialists aforementioned.

There will be printed news-letters issued by this organization, though the format and frequency of publication, is still under consideration. The name Space Review will be retained.

Present officers of the IFSB will eventually receive a letter regarding our new organization and its policies, as soon as all details are worked out.

We wish to thank one and all for their courtesy and cooperation and interest in making the IFSB a succes . We wish every success to the other groups organized to solve the saucer mystery.

We sincerely hope that the interest shown IFSB will be shown to our new organization.

EXECUTIVE STAFF — IFSB

Place
Stamp
Here

To:

I.F.S.B.

P.O. BOX 241

BRIDGEPORT 2, CONN.

U.S.A.

TO ALL SUBSCRIBER-MEMBERS

Since this is your last issue of Space Review, we wish your cooperation in reading carefully the following:

If there is any refund due you as a subscriber-member it will be noted at the bottom of this page.

These figures have been checked carefully, but if you feel there is a discrepancy please mention the initials of the checker, along with your membership number, when writing about same.

Refunds will be mailed as soon as possible.

If. in place of a refund you desire some back issues of Space Review provisions for receiving same are noted below. Copies of back issues will be mailed as long as the supply lasts.

If, in place of refunds or back issues, you desire your name to be placed on the mailing list of our new organization, provisions for noting same are made below. Those choosing this latter method will receive copies of all news-letters, published by our new organization, up to the expiration of their present membership date.

IT IS VERY IMPORTANT THAT POST CARD BELOW IS MAILED IN TO US AT YOUR EARLIEST CONVENIENCE. YOUR COOPERATION WILL BE GREATLY APPRECIATED.

ALL MEMBERS WISHING A REFUND WILL SEND BACK TO US THEIR MEMBERSHIP CARD ALONG WITH THE FORM BELOW.

Membership No...................... Date Joined...

Amount Received...................... Issues Space Review You Have Received......................

Issues Due You...................... Refund Due You...................... Checked by......................

Please check one of the following:

............Please place my name on the mailing list of your new organization.

............Please send me back issues of Space Review for number of issues due me.

............Please send me refund due me.

....
Signature of Subscriber-Member

We wish to thank all persons sending in articles for Space Review and we hope to use excerpts from same from time to time.

Space Review

SINCE 1952

"A SCIENCE NEWS-LETTER"
P. O. BOX 241
BRIDGEPORT 4, CONN.
————U. S. A.————

Vol. III No. 1   FEBRUARY---1954   — A LIMITED AND RESTRICTED PUBLICATION

What is the universe? It is the greatest mystery of all time and it is a mystery that will never be solved.

Every year, newer and finer astronomical instruments are being perfected, yet each of these instruments will have a limit to its efficiency. Since the universe is limitless it will be, without a doubt, a losing struggle. It is true that every year new and greater discoveries will be made in the universe, but it is too much to hope for miracles.

The untiring efforts of our astronomers are rewarding. The study of astronomy today is vastly different than it was ages ago. At that time it was looked upon as foolishness and astronomers were called fools, but today it is looked upon as necessary and astronomers are respected.

Space travel will be the first stepping stone and the moon will be the most logical step. Although more is known about the moon than any other heavenly body it is the actual physical exploration that will give us the knowledge we are seeking.

After the moon has been reached, possession will belong to the first ones setting foot upon it. It will be vastly different than staking a small claim on earth, consisting of a number of acres, since it will be a complete earth claimed as a whole.

After the exploration comes colonization and interplanetary travel between the earth and its satellite. When we have spanned the 238,857 miles to the moon it will be a tremendous step forward into space.

Years will roll by before the next problem will arise. This problem will be the reaching of new frontiers, either the planet VENUS or MARS. Which shall it be?

Will they attempt a trip to Venus, the next nearest body, which is shrouded in mystery, since one can only speculate on what lies beneath its dense, warm clouds, or would they make Mars their goal, a planet about which more is known.

When astronomers reach the moon, they will no doubt set up an observatory to study these two bodies. The atmosphere on the moon will be much more favorable for clearer observation. It is then they will determine which of the two they will visit first.

Most of our generation will see the reaching of the moon, but that is as far as they will get in our generation, and maybe for some generations to come unless a miracle occurs.

****

Recently Drew Pearson mentioned in his column that the Air Force will scan Mars when the planet nears earth this spring. He went on to say that ".....the Air Force will send high-flying observation planes and guided missiles into the upper atmosphere for a clearer look.........when Mars will approach nearer to the earth than at any time in the last thirteen years. In addition a scientific expedition will journey to Bloemfontein, South Africa, which will be the closest point on earth from which to observe our neighbor planet". This, in our opinion, is a great step forward and we are certain that much new information will be obtained.

****

As all astronomers know, the earth and the planets making up our solar system revolve about the central body, the sun. However, scientists and astronomers both claim that there are millions of such solar systems in the universe. If this be true, then can we speculate that all of these solar systems revolve about a central pivot or body such as our sun? Perhaps each solar system has its own orbit to follow. Considering the aspects of this statement we would like the opinions of others, and would be pleased to hear from anyone.

MARS IS THE PLANET TO WATCH IN 1954

Mars will be visible some time during the hours of darkness every night throughout the year 1954.

It will start the year as a none-too-conspicuous object, increase to great brilliancy until June and then gradually decrease, but still remain very bright until the end of the year.

In June it will be in "opposition" to the sun. That means that the earth, constantly gaining on Mars in their race around the sun, will catch up with the planet on June 24 and the two objects will then be in a straight line from the sun, with Mars on the night side of the earth and the sun on the daylight side.

If Mars and the earth went around the sun in perfect circles, the two would always be at the same distance from each other at the times of opposition, but they travel in ellipses of different forms.

This year, the opposition will be the closest we have had since 1941, but in 1956, the opposition will be almost the closest possible. These distances can vary from more than sixty million miles to less than 35 million miles. This year, the distance will be a little over forty million miles.

Oppositions of Mars always occur when it is going through its "retrograde" (apparently backward) motion------an illusion which we get on the earth because we are passing Mars in space.

This year the retrograde loop of Mars will be particularly interesting to watch because it will carry the brilliant planet through the stars of the conspicuous and well-known formation in Sagittarius which we call the Teapot.

From mid April to May 23, we will see the planet pass above the lid of the Teapot. Then it will seem to reverse direction and move backward through the lid, reaching opposition June 24 when it is beginning to move across the Teapot's spout.

This illusion of backward motion will end July 30 and Mars will resume its normal course eastward, to pass again through the lid during the first half of September and leave the Teapot behind after the middle of that month.

(Courtesy Hayden Planetarium "The Sky Reporter")
****

THE RED PLANET-----In astronomy, Mars is the fourth of the planets revolving about the sun. Its orbit is completely outside that of our earth and its mean distance from the sun is 141,500,000 miles. The year of Mars is 687 earth days making the Martian seasons twice as long as ours in duration.
An Italian astronomer, Giovanni Virginio Schiaparelli, observed strange markings on the planet in 1872 which he called "canali" which meant channels in his language. This has been twisted through the years to the present word "canals". His name was given to one of the canals. The canals were also observed by Percival Lowell who expressed the belief that they were built by an intelligent race of beings who constructed them to bring water from the poles. Some observers report seeing vegetation along the sides of these canals. It is believed that the polar caps melt at a certain time of the year. The existance of vegetation, which changes color from green to brown, like our earth's summer and autumn, has led many to believe that life could exist there

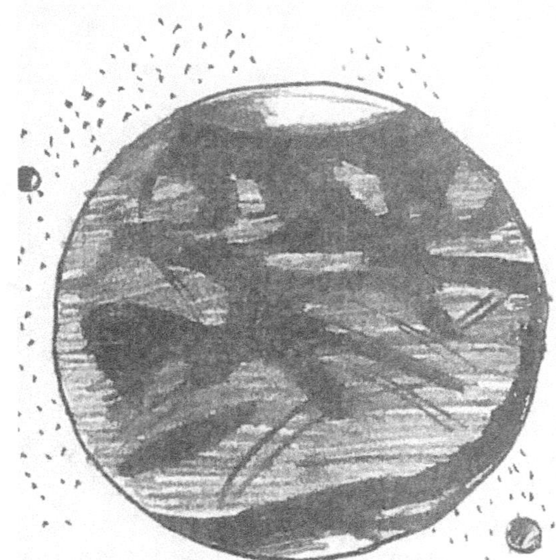

"LET'S GET ACQUAINTED WITH THE PLANET MARS"

Fourth of the planets in the solar system.
Distance from the Sun in miles---141,600,000.
Distance from the Earth in miles---
                    At furthest point------62,900,000
                    At nearest point--------34,600,000
Diameter----------4220 miles.
Color of Planet through telescopes----reddish.
Mass of weight compared to earth---0.11.
Volume compared to earth------------0.15.
Number of moons--------2 (two) Deimos and Phobos.
Length of Day----------687 days.
Temperatures------Reach 50 degrees F. near the
                      equator.
Diameter of Mars Moons------10 miles.
Physical Description-- Has white polar caps.
Greenish blue areas, reddish brown areas at differen
times during the year. Atmosphere is mostly carbon dioxide with traces of oxygen. Has
peculiar markings resembling canals. (See page two). Revolutions--24 hrs., 37 min.,22.58
seconds. Clouds on Mars----vary from red, white, and blue in color.

****

ODD STORIES ABOUT MARS

On January 16, 1950, a Japanese astronomer in Osaka, Japan claims to have seen a mushroom shaped cloud or explosion on Mars, similar to our atomic explosions. Many said it
might have been a race of people testing a bomb like ours, or it might have been the result
of a space ship taking off from the planet. However, scientists say it was a volcanic explosion, and the case rests at that.

****

Some believe that Mars may have intelligent life living in lid covered cities.

****

Starting from the furthest planet from the Sun, Pluto, and working in toward the Sun,
it is believed that all of the planets may have been inhabited at one time or another and
that as the sun began to burn out of its full strength, life either died or migrated to
another world when life became unbearable.
Mars may now be in its final stages, water supply diminishing and the atmosphere becoming thin. Its people are either dead or so intelligent that they are building space
craft to find a new world to live.
Earth is as Mars was at one time, but will some day suffer the same conditions. Venus
is now in the prehistoric stage similar to earth's earlier stages, and that no doubt accoun
for the fog and heavy mist that shrouds the planet in mystery. It is a steaming jungle.
Mercury is too hot for life and may cool off as Venus is doing now, and support life in the
final days of the sun's existence.

****

The inner moon of Mars revolves so fast that it rises and sets three times during the
Martian Day.

****

Large dust storms on the desert portions of Mars have led scientists to believe that a
large movement of some sort was being made over the desert region since the storm or dust
moved off at a great distance rather than localize its force.

****

"NOT UNTIL MAN HAS PROBED TO THE END OF SPACE WILL HIS KNOWLEDGE HAVE REACHED ITS EXTREMITY

"SPACE REVIEW REVIEWS RECENT BOOKS"

OUR NEIGHBOUR WORLDS----V.A.Firsoff, M.A.
>Philosophical Library, 15 E. 40th Street, New York 16,
>New York. Price--$6.00. Illustrated profusely.

****EXCELLENT***

Academic books on astronomy written in a manner to kill
even the most enthusiastic interest are common enough;
so are accounts of inter-planetary travel in which the
author's enthusiasm outruns his judgment and knowledge,
both of which are sometimes scanty. In OUR NEIGHBOUR
WORLDS a fully qualified and practical astronomer writes
graphically and readably on things he knows or has good
reason for believing, and there is never any possible
confusion between definite knowledge and personal opinion.

"OUR NEIGHBOUR WORLDS is a visit to outer space that en-
thralls the reader".

****

SPACE TRAVEL---(An Illustrated Survey of its Problems and Prospects)
>Kenneth W. Gatland and Anthony M. Kunesch
>Philosophical Library, 15 E. 40th Street, New York 16,
>New York. Price--$4.75.

****EXCELLENT***

Are you interested in visiting Mars? The answers to this
question might be various, but in the minds of the authors
there is no possible doubt. They are; and they know exactly how to get tthere. Both Mr. Junesch and Mr. Gatland are
technical experts in their own fields, and the latter is
also secretary of the once derided British Interplanetary
Society.

The illustration, as may be imagined, form an integral
part of the book. There are nearly 100 of them.

****

DEVELOPMENT OF THE GUIDED MISSILE------Kenneth W. Gatland
>Philosophical Library, 15 E. 40th Street, New York 16,
>New York. Price--$3.75. Illustrated.

GOOD

The substance of this book was originally published as a
series of articles in FLIGHT during the summer of 1951,
and the decision to reprint the material in more permanent
form is an indication of the interest which the subject
now commands among technical people.

This is more of a book for technical-minded people and
those seriously interested in the study and history of
space missiles. "An Evening Well Spent With This Book".

****

Space Review

SINCE 1952

"A SCIENCE NEWS-LETTER"
P. O. BOX 241
BRIDGEPORT 4, CONN.
————U. S. A.————

VOL. III NO. II   APRIL---1954   — A LIMITED AND RESTRICTED PUBLICATION

<u>ARE WE LIVING ON BORROWED TIME?</u>

Many people wonder just how secure we are on this planet known as Earth. Writers through the years have expressed their opinions in this matter and many of their theories are discussed here.

The idea of a hydrogen bomb war in our present day, is foremost in the ways in which the Earth could be destroyed. Man could very likely bring about the destruction of Earth. The destruction and havoc from hydrogen bombs would be vast, but the contamination of the atmosphere may be even greater. Yet man is still comtemplating an even more powerful weapon than the hydrogen bomb, when they discuss the dreaded cobalt bomb. This could lead to the annihilation of all mankind. If the first cobalt bomb is dropped it may very likely be the last cobalt bomb.

The possibility of the sun exploding would destroy not only the Earth but the entire solar system.

The sun might burn itself out, and Earth and other planets will become balls of frozen matter.

The planets of the solar system keep their positions by a mutual pull of all for each other. If by chance this attraction was increased or decreased, some planets, if not all, could go hurtling out into space or fall into the sun.

What would happen if the Earth suddenly stopped rotating on its axis? It would be either day or night on one side of the planet. The side facing the sun would boil beneath its rays and the opposite side would fine temperatures below zero. It would be another ice age.

A comet or meteor could suddenly strike the Earth and not only cause tremendous destruction, but may also throw the planet out of its orbit and send it into space.

If our nearest planet, the moon, should lose its attraction it might very well fall to the Earth by the gravitational pull of our planet.

Some of the people of today do not know that the ice caps of the Earth in the polar regions are increasing in size and may suddenly capsize the Earth. The Earth is becoming top heavy and when it gets too heavy it will tip to balance itself.

Another possibility would be the sudden cessation of rain or moisture in our atmosphere. This would eventually result in a vast desert and everyone would die.

In summing up all of the above, we might add that some of the above may not happen for billions of years, some may not happen for millions of years, and others may happen <u>THIS YEAR.</u>

THE PITTED WINDSHIELDS AND EYEGLASSES

Recently in Seattle, Washington and other western cities the populace reported that the windshields of their automobiles and also eyeglasses, were pitted by a strange black substance that alighted on same. Scientists poo-pooed the idea that it was caused by the recent hydrogen bomb tests. They made tests of the chemical and found that it did not contain any radioactive material. However, more recently than that, a scientist claims that some of the material removed from the convertible top of an auto had radioactive ingredients. So, it appears that the H-Bomb must have been responsible for this strange occurence. It is time that we woke up to the fact that the H-Bomb and the A-Bomb are not toys and should be abandoned as a destructive weapon. Man will learn too late of the power he has harnessed and then what can we do about it.

****

EXCERPT FROM RECENT LETTER TO "SPACE REVIEW" IN REGARDS TO ARTICLE IN FEBRUARY ISSUE.

"And I was not surprised to see a mention of the "atmosphere of the moon". It is not possible for the moon to have an atmosphere of any extent, and probably has none at all (unless you would call a few ions of Argon an atmosphere). Instead of an advantage, that may make it impossible to have a sizeable observatory on the moon. This is because there would be nothing to prevent the meteoric dust from hitting the surface at high velocity, and thus pitting the telescopic lense or mirror. The seriousness of this depends upon the concentration of the high-velocity dust.

The question concerning a super-solar system has been answered by astronomers for years. The galactic system is composed of individual stars, star systems, clusters, etc. that revolve around the galactic center. And above these are the supergalactic systems, composed of groups of galaxies. The next highest unit that we know of is the universe itself, which is expanding from a central point, wherever it is."

(Thanks to the contributor)

****

THE MYSTERY PLANET---VENUS

Venus is the second planet in order of distance from the sun. More closely like Earth than any other body in the solar system, its mean distance from the sun is 67,200,000 miles. It completes one complete revolution about the sun in 224.7 days. The planet is completely covered by a blanket of vaporous clouds and makes observation almost impossible. At times through the telescope they have noted shaded areas and white areas. Of course they are not certain if this is the surface or just clouds they have seen. Venus has no moons and therefore must have a very dark night. Some think that the planet Mercury might have at one time been the moon of Venus, but was swept away by the sun. It is believed that Venus has large snow caps similar to our Earth. There is no reason why intelligent life could not exist on the planet Venus, because to deny this is not commonsense, but merely a manifestation.

(Last line from--OUR NEIGHBOUR WORLDS)

****

"WE ARE NOW LIVING IN THE AGE OF UNCERTAINTY. ONE NEVER KNOWS WHAT WILL HAPPEN IN THE NEXT SECOND".

<u>OUR NEAREST NEIGHBOR</u>

Our satellite, the moon, is one of the most interesting bodies in the universe. It has been a subject for discussion for thousands of years. Since it is our nearest neighbor we should know much more about it than we do at the present time. It is not surrounded by clouds which makes it easier to observe than other planets.

The features of the moon can be observed by the naked eye which is not possible with other planets. The craters, the most obvious features, are still a subject of contraversy. The majority of the astronomers claim that these craters were caused by meteors hitting at terrific speed. A few have claimed that the moon might have been inhabited at one time by a race superior to that of Earth. This race of people, these scientists contend, destroyed themselves in a great war. They supposedly used weapons much more powerful than our atom or hydrogen bombs, and it was these weapons that caused the craters.

If we were to take a trip to our neighbor the moon, at the mere rate of 200 miles per hour, it would take a little more than a month and a half. However, life on the moon would be quite a problem since there is no atmosphere and not a drop of water.

If there were water on the moon, the Earth would affect their tides, just as the moon effects ours. It is suspected that if this were the case it has acted as a brake and has slowed down the rotation of the moon. This could also be taking place with the Earth, and in time, with the days lengthening, our day may become as long as a month. If this should happen, the Earth may someday always have one side facing the moon.

One of the most mysterious things about the moon in recent years, has been the observation of strange glowing lights seen shining on the surface of the satellite.

A few years ago, contact was made with the moon by use of radar. The signal bounced back to the senders.

It is believed that the moon is a rich source of valuable minerals, and the nation reaching this heavenly body first, will come into possession of all these resources. The problem then, would be, how to remove them to Earth, or if the process of refining could be accomplished on the moon itself.

It is suspected that gold may be the most common ore found there, and if this is true, gold would be as valuable as water is on Earth.

The people on Earth only see one side of the moon, since the other side is always facing away from the Earth.

It is almost foolish to contemplate trips to Mars and Venus before the moon has been reached, or has it been reached already????

There will be a great many revelations coming forth in the near future that will astound everyone.

The moon is no longer as mysterious as we are led to believe! It bears watching.

****

"THE SECRETS OF THE UNIVERSE WILL SOMEDAY BE THE UNDOING OF ALL MANKIND"

"MANKIND WILL SOMEDAY FIND THE SECRETS OF THE UNIVERSE AND WILL NOT BE ABLE TO COPE WITH THEM"

"SPACE REVIEW REVIEWS RECENT SCIENCE BOOKS"

YOUR TRIP INTO SPACE------Lynn Poole, Producer, John Hopkins TV Science Review, Whittlesey House, McGraw Hill Book Co. Inc., 330 W. 42nd St., New York 36, N. Y. Price---$2.75 Illustrated by Clifford Geary.

Fascinating, accurate information about what space travel actually will mean to every one of us. How soon can we reasonably expect to travel into space? What kind of accommodations will take us there? What are the dangers we will have to face? What do scientists say we will find when we break through into outer space? And, perhaps most important----what will be the effect of this trip on everyone on Earth? hese and many more important questions are answered with authority in this book.

The illustrations though simply drawn are very expressive in giving the required detail necessary.

"A Fascinating Science Course in Itself".

VERY GOOD

****

THE COMPLETE BOOK OF OUTER SPACE----Published by Maco Magazine Corporation, 480 Lexington Ave., New York 17, New York. Price $.75 (Magazine Type). Illustrated profusely.

A magazine composed of outstanding articles by equally outstanding authors. Some of these authors are: Willy Ley: Dr. Wernher Von Braun; Dr. Heinz Haber; Hugo Gernsback and every other top expert.

We recommend especially the article by Dr. Heinz Haber, Dept. of Space Medicine, Randolph Field, which is titled "Space Medicine". "This Little Magazine is Well Worth the "Space" it Takes Up".

VERY GOOD

****

THE CONQUEST OF SPACE------Text by Willy Ley; Paintings by Chesley Bonestell Published by Viking Press, 18 E. 48th St., New York 17, N. Y. Price--$3.95.

In the Conquest of Space the collaborators portray in text and pictures the universe our children may someday visit.
To mention just a few of the places on the itinerary we visit the mts. of the moon, Venus and other planets. We see Jupiter from its large moon, the landscapes of Mars, and a planet of the double star Mira.
"The Viking Press has in printing the above book, printed a record of space information that will remain a collector's item".

EXCELLENT

****

OUR NEXT ISSUE WILL BE OUT SOMETIME IN THE MONTH OF JULY OR THEREABOUTS---PLEASE SEND US YOUR COMMENTS.

Space Review

SINCE 1952

"A SCIENCE NEWS-LETTER"

P. O. BOX 241

BRIDGEPORT 4, CONN.

——————U. S. A.——————
——————U.   A.——————

VOL. III No. III   AUGUST 1954   A LIMITED AND RESTRICTED PUBLICATION

SPACE REVIEW PREDICTS THE FUTURE

THE YEAR 1955: Predictions
     YEAR

In the year ninetten hundred fifty five many things will take place in the field of science.
It will be a year marked by great discoveries as well as a year marked by strange develop-
ments in the heavens. The year will be one that will make history, more so than any other
year, since the birth of Christ.

A cure for dreaded cancer will surely make medical annals, and a step toward the cure for
heart disease shall fall soon after.

A strange phenomena in the skies will prove to be a step toward conquering the mysteries of
space and the universe.

Noah's ark shall be found by explorers and the inside of the ark shall reveal strange writings,
which when translated shall throw new light upon what took place at that time.

The weather will bring terrible destruction to many parts of the world. A strange rumbling
in the Arctic regions will cause much concern among our scientists. Heat of unknown intensity
will make living on the North Eastern coast of the United States almost unbearable, while the
Southern part of United States will be amazed at the bitter cold and snow that they will have
to undergo during the winter months. England will experience a complete change in weather
than what it has been accustomed. Earthquakes, tidal waves, hurricanes and tornadoes shall
make the headlines with many lives lost.

A three letter word shall loom into the headlines toward Christmas time of 1955. It shall
be a word that we do not like.

A strange illness will strike in the North American continent in which the eyes shall be
affected in thousands of humans.

Science shall announce a great discovery from one of our leading observatories. It will make
headlines in the newspapers of the world.

Telephones shall be equipped with television screens, but the installation shall be enormous
in cost.

Laws governing birth control will be brought up by the Federal government and it will end up
as a world discussion at the U.N.

A weapon more deadly than the Cobalt bomb will be announced.

An automobile will be designed that shall revolutionize the industry. It will mean a complete
change in the production of all motor cars.

Railroads shall announce great strides in improving their facilities.

A famous explorer will make a startling discovery at the North Pole.

TRUE OR FALSE STATEMENTS

Everyone has a curiosity that will eventually get them into all sorts of trouble, but we are all entitled to express our own opinions in this land of freedom of the press. However, at times it might get you into some difficulty, but when that happens you must cope with it and use your better judgment by abiding with the rules.

The future holds much for the people of the world and many of us will be astounded if we only knew some of the things that are no doubt taking place at this very moment. Many wild ideas are being expressed in magazines and periodicals, but although they all sound fantastic, many of them are based on some little leak of information that may have reached the ears of the right person.

We are living in an age of not only survival of the fittest, but also survival of the strongest and most advanced.

Nations will compete against each other to gain new heights in weapons of destruction, as well as advancements in science.

Many of the statements we read in books, magazines, and newspapers are either true or false, but we are left to figure out which it might be, as they use double talk to throw us off our course. Here are a few statements that you might look upon and decide for yourself whether they are actually sound or unsound.

1. UNITED STATES HAS ESTABLISHED A BASE ON THE MOON. This base was set up in 1947 and has been growing in size. By use of radar and radio guided objects they keep in close contact with bases on the Earth itself. Those that volunteered to go were soldiers and scientists without any families or dependents for security purposes. The billions of dollars spent for atom research was not all used for that purpose, as much of the money was used to set up and keep the base operating, known as Project Luna.

2. RUSSIA HAS REACHED THE MOON AND IS PREPARING LAUNCHING SITES FOR SUPER ROCKETS. The Soviet Union has reached the moon with the aid of German Scientists who went over to their side after World War II. Since world domination is the policy of Russia, they plan to use the moon as a real launching station for super rockets aimed at the free democratic nations. It is this project that keeps Russia so arrogant and unafraid.

3. A SUPER DEVICE HAS BEEN INVENTED BY A WORLD POWER THAT WILL SURPASS ANY TYPE OF AIR-CRAFT ON THE EARTH.

4. THE UNITED STATES GOVERNMENT IS CONCEALING SOMETHING SO FANTASTIC THAT EVEN THEY ARE AFRAID TO REVEAL IT TO THE PUBLIC.

5. RUSSIA IS PLANNING ON A NON-DESTRUCTIVE WAR USING A SPECIAL GAS THAT WILL PUT ALL THE VICTIMS TO SLEEP UNTIL THEY FULLY TAKE OVER THE COUNTRY INTACT. THE GAS WILL BE SPREAD BY A STRANGE GUIDED OBJECT OF CIRCULAR SHAPE.

These are just a few of the statements that you may see from time to time, and they will not only startle you, but make you wonder if what is printed is really true or false. Well, we will leave that up to you to decide. Your guess is as good as ours, and we hope that ours is the wrong one.

****

(Quotations may not be made from the above article without our express permission).

****

PARTICLE FROM SPACE HELD AS EVIDENCE OF "MATTER IN REVERSE"

By RENNIE TAYLOR, Associated Press Science Reporter

The first substantial evidence of the existence of stable "matter in reverse"----a particle from outer space which anihilates the basic material of all earthly substances ----has been found by a University of Chicago scientist.

From somewhere out in the Milky Way or perhaps from some more distant island universe this strange bit of matter came to the top of the earth's atmosphere last winter. With tremendous energy it struck an aluminum covered film pack being carried by a cosmic ray research balloon high over Texas.

The space particle went through the film pack like a bullet through a deck of cards. In doing so it produced a scientifically thrilling sequence of what appears to be the conversion of earthly matter into energy and then a reconversion of this energy into another form of earthly matter.

A report of the event was ade before a meeting of the American Physical society here yesterday by its discoverer, Dr. Marcel Schein, one of this country's foremost cosmic ray scientists.

Dr. Schein said the only conclusion he could make so far was that the strange visitor was something which nuclear scientists have been seeking for years---an anti-proton.

The term anti-proton is an exciting word even among atom scientists. It is their way of describing the basic particle out of which reverse matter presumably is made. This is called "contra-terrene matter", or "matter against the earth".

Theoretically an anti-proton is the counterpart or opposite number of a proton. The proton is the core of the hydrogen atom and the main substance out of which all ordinary matter is made.

When an anti-proton and a proton collide they presumably destroy each other. That apparently was what happened, Dr. Schein said, when the space visitor hit the film pack. It collided with a proton in the aluminum covering of the film pack.

For scientists the implications are far-reaching. They suggest that somewhere in the universe there exists a means of annihilating or converting into energy all the various kinds of matter known on earth.

It also lends support to something else which scientists long have suspected--that somewhere within the realm of creation there may be forms of matter made entirely of contraterrene particles.

To co   that picture at least one more "reverse" particle would be needed---an antineutron. This would be the counterpart of the neutron as we know it---the companion particle which with the proton is contained in all earthly substances except simple hydrogen.

There is no danger that anyone will corral a lot of anti-protons and destroy the planet. They are too scarce and hard to handle. If they ever are produced artificially they will come only from the biggest atom smashing machines and will be used to check nuclear theories. In this way they could lead to a new understanding of matter and perhaps great benefits with new forms of atomic energy.

SPECIAL ANNOUNCEMENT TO ALL READERS:

For a long time many science fans and also science fiction fans have been searching for
a recording of the Orson Welles' Broadcast of the early 30's that frightened the nation.
It was a radio adaptation of "War of the Worlds" by H.G.Wells. Such realistic broadcasting
gave late tuner-inners a scare that caused some deaths. Now this broadcast is available
to all those that own long-playing phonographs. For those interested please write to the
following address: Dauntless International, 225 Lafayette Street, New York 12, New York.
"War of the Worlds"----Audio Masterpiece LPA-2355---Price---$5.95.

****

A FINE NEW BOOK BY JOHN WILEY AND SONS INC.

"PHYSICAL METEOROLOGY"----by John C. Johnson, Published by John Wiley and Sons, Inc.
                        440 Fourth Avenue, New York 16, New York. Profusely illustrated,
                        Price--$7.50.

          Physical Meteorology performs a notable service by bringing to-
          gether, in a single volume, a comprehensive picture of this new
          branch of knowledge which in a comparatively short time has
          assumed great, and growing, importance in a number of fields.

          The book is planned to serve a dual purpose. It is designed to
          meet the needs of research workers in the many fields in which
          t   sphere plays a significant role. At the same time, it
          is planned to fill the requirements of professional meteorological
          courses at the college level and of students taking the subject
                  elective in other curricula. The work presupposes no spec-
              ackground beyond basic physics and mathematics including
          differential and integral calculus.

          Among the many important features of the work is the first organ-
          ized scientific presentation of the physical and meteorological
          concepts on which the modern attempts at rain-making are based.
          Valuable, too, is the extensive bibliographical material provided.
          This covers not only the original sources and important surveys,
          but also most recent additions to the literature.

          The author is a graduate of Middlebury College in Vermont, Mass.
          Institute of Technology, Served in the United States Air Force,
          and at present is working on a weather radar project in the
          Research Laboratory of Physical Electronics at Tufts College.

          "For the advanced student this is an invaluable piece of liter-
          ature. It's contents are priceless, and it's concept is one
          of the finest to date on the subject that it unfolds to the
          reader". Space Review full-heartedly suggests that all science-
          minded folk add this volume to their bookshelves.

****

THE NEXT ISSUE OF SPACE REVIEW WILL NOT BE OUT UNTIL THE LATTER PART OF OCTOBER, 1954.

****

When you order items from this page, please mention that you saw the ad
in Space Review.